Shifting Fortunes

Shifting Fortunes

The Perils of the Growing American Wealth Gap

Chuck Collins
Betsy Leondar-Wright
Holly Sklar

United for a Fair Economy

Research Assistance: Chris Hartman, Scott Klinger, Bonnie Shulman
Cover, Design and Layout: Chris Hartman

ISBN 0-9659249-2-0

Printed in the United States

Published by United for a Fair Economy, 37 Temple Place, Boston, MA 02111. www.stw.org

10 9 8 7 6 5 4 3 2 1

Contents

Tables and Figures

Foreword
By Lester Thurow

Market economies can adjust to any distribution of wealth and earnings. If the top has more wealth and earnings and the broad middle of the distribution has less, the market simply produces more of the goods and services wanted by those at the top and fewer of the goods and services wanted by those in the middle. Firms serving middle class consumers move upscale or downscale—or, if they cannot do either, they go out of business.

In the hard-nosed "survival of the fittest" version of capitalism (to use a phrase invented by a 19th century economist, Spencer, and borrowed by Darwin for use in his masterpiece on evolution), individuals who cannot compete are supposed to starve and go out of business too. That threat and that reality is part of the motivation that makes the system efficient.

In the theology of capitalism the distributions of wealth, income and earnings are of no consequence. There is no concept of fairness other than that those who produce in the market get fairly compensated by the market. Those who do not produce are shoved aside by the market. They do not get to consume—they do not deserve to consume.

The problems are political. How does one put together a democracy based on the concept of equality while running an economy with ever greater degrees of economic inequality? At some point, those who are losing economically have to use their political power to vote in a government that reverses the outcome of the market. No one knows where this point is. In the United States there have now been over 25 years of rising inequality in income and wealth with no observable political backlashes. Perhaps our society could move much farther along the continuum toward inequality; perhaps not. But it is a stupid society that runs an experiment to see where its breaking points are.

In the past, egalitarian democracy has been coupled with inegalitarian capitalism on the assumption that government would do three things. First, government guaranteed that first-class educations and skills would be available to children of parents who did not have first-class income and wealth. The next generation would be better skilled and able to earn more than the last. Second, it would insure that those who cannot compete for whatever reason do not get driven into economic extinction (hence the social safety net). Third, government would use the tax system to make after-tax distributions of income and wealth more equal than before-tax distributions of income and wealth. For the last two decades, the American government has been backing away from all three of those commitments.

Americans are used to discussions about what is fair between rich and poor. What you are about to read is not just a discussion about what is happening to the rich and what is happening to the poor. It is also a discussion about what is happening to middle Americans—those who are neither in the top 10 percent of the population nor the bottom 10 percent of the population. As you are about to see, they are big losers over the last 25 years. Their wealth and earnings are falling as a share of the total wealth and earnings in the United States. More disturbingly, their wealth and earnings have been falling absolutely in inflation-corrected dollars. They have less than they used to have despite an economy that has dramatically increased the per capita Gross Domestic Product.

Put simply and bluntly, the great American middle class has become a non-participant in the American dream. A grand old species is becoming extinct.

Lester Thurow is professor of management and economics at the MIT Sloan School of Management and the author of numerous books including The Future of Capitalism.

Foreword
By Juliet Schor

The official economic news is exuberant: We are in the midst of the nation's longest peacetime expansion, unemployment is disappearing, the stock market is defying gravity, consumer confidence has soared. Luxuries once reserved for the wealthy are now middle class mainstays, as households remodel their kitchens, tool around town in their spanking new sport utility vehicles, and generally live the good life. Capitalism has been kind to us.

While this picture has superficial appeal (after all, the roads are clogged with SUVs), the official discourse has a profoundly disturbing, almost Orwellian dimension. It describes the experience of the privileged minority that is doing spectacularly well. In a bizarre twist of logic, the news has been good because the punditocracy admits only good news.

Shifting Fortunes completes the picture. It reveals that financial security has become more elusive for most families and that the economic boom has been built on the sweat of the 30 percent of American workers who earn poverty or near-poverty wages. Underlying these trends is an inescapable fact: our economy has been getting increasingly unequal. Whether measured by wages, income or wealth, for 25 years the share of the privileged has increased, and everyone else (a roughly 80 percent majority) has become relatively worse off. We are truly in a second Gilded Age.

Why does inequality matter? Some argue that it doesn't: All we need to worry about is the absolute level of material well-being. Economic growth is the solution, they say, to the problems of poverty and low incomes. There are two flaws to this popular view. First, growth no longer has the magical quality of benefiting everyone—in recent years, growth has actually been associated with the immiseration of a whole group of workers. And second, the idea that the distribution of income is irrelevant is not supported by the scholarly evidence. It seems that relative position does matter.

Health, well-being and satisfaction appear to be heavily influenced by the ways in which economic resources, prestige and social position are distributed. In more unequal societies, human well-being and quality of life appear to be lower, for a variety of reasons needing more research.

The reasons may not turn out to be so very complicated. Humans are social. We judge our own situations very much in comparison to others around us. It is not surprising that people experience less stress, more peace of mind and feel happier in an environment with more social cohesion and more equality. Perhaps it's time to make that conclusion a fundamental basis of our economic and social policy.

Juliet Schor is an economist and senior lecturer on women's studies at Harvard University and the author of The Overspent American.

1

Overview: The Growing Wealth Gap

Behind the hoopla of the booming nineties, most Americans have actually lost wealth. Most households have lower net worth (assets minus debt) than they did in 1983, when the stock market began its record-breaking climb. From 1983 to 1998, the stock market grew a cumulative 1,336 percent.[1] The wealthiest households reaped most of the gains.

The top 1 percent of households have soared while most Americans have been working harder to stay in place, if they have not fallen further behind. Since the 1970s, the top 1 percent of households have doubled their share of the national wealth at the expense of everyone else. Using data from the Federal Reserve Survey of Consumer Finances, economist Edward Wolff of New York University says that the top 1 percent had 40 percent of the nation's household wealth as of 1997. The top 1 percent of households have more wealth than the entire bottom 95 percent.

Financial wealth is even more concentrated. The top 1 percent of households have nearly half of all financial wealth (net worth minus net equity in owner-occupied housing).[2] Wealth is further concentrated at the top of the top 1 percent. The richest 1/2 percent of households have 42 percent of the financial wealth.[3]

Between 1983 and 1995, the inflation-adjusted net worth of the top 1 percent swelled by 17 percent. The bottom 40 percent of households lost an astounding 80 percent. Their net worths shrunk from $4,400 to an even more meager $900. The middle fifth of Americans lost over 11 percent. Only the

Figure I
The Wealth Gap

Distribution of Net Worth, 1997

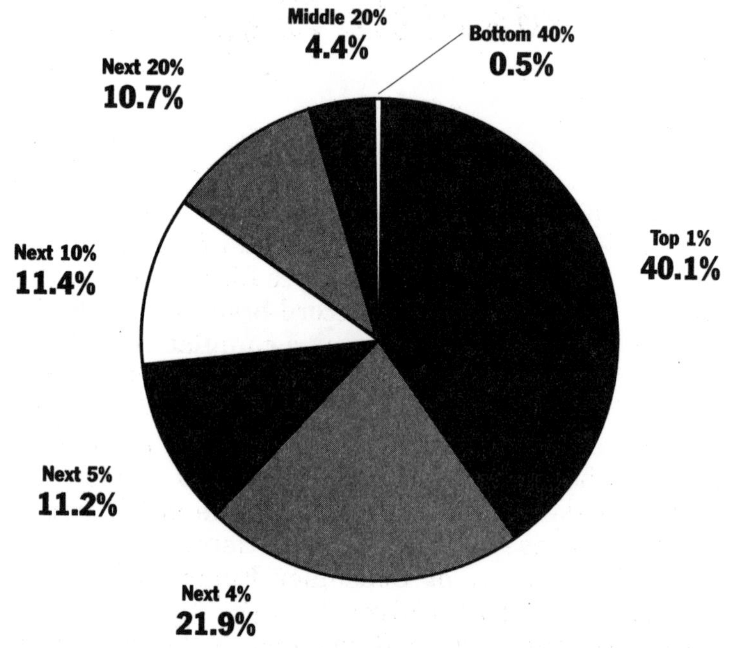

Source: Edward Wolff, "Recent Trends in Wealth Ownership," 1998, based on Federal Reserve Survey of Consumer Finances. Figures for 1997 are preliminary.

top 5 percent gained any net worth in this period. The top 5 percent now have more than 60 percent of all household wealth.[4]

Adjusting for inflation, the net worth of the household in the middle (the median household) fell from $54,600 in 1989 to $45,600 in 1995, before rising again to a projected $49,900 in 1997. That's still $4,700 lower than the median net worth a decade ago. Median financial wealth has fallen from $13,000 in 1989 to a projected $11,700 in 1997.[5]

Figure 2
Only the Rich Got Richer

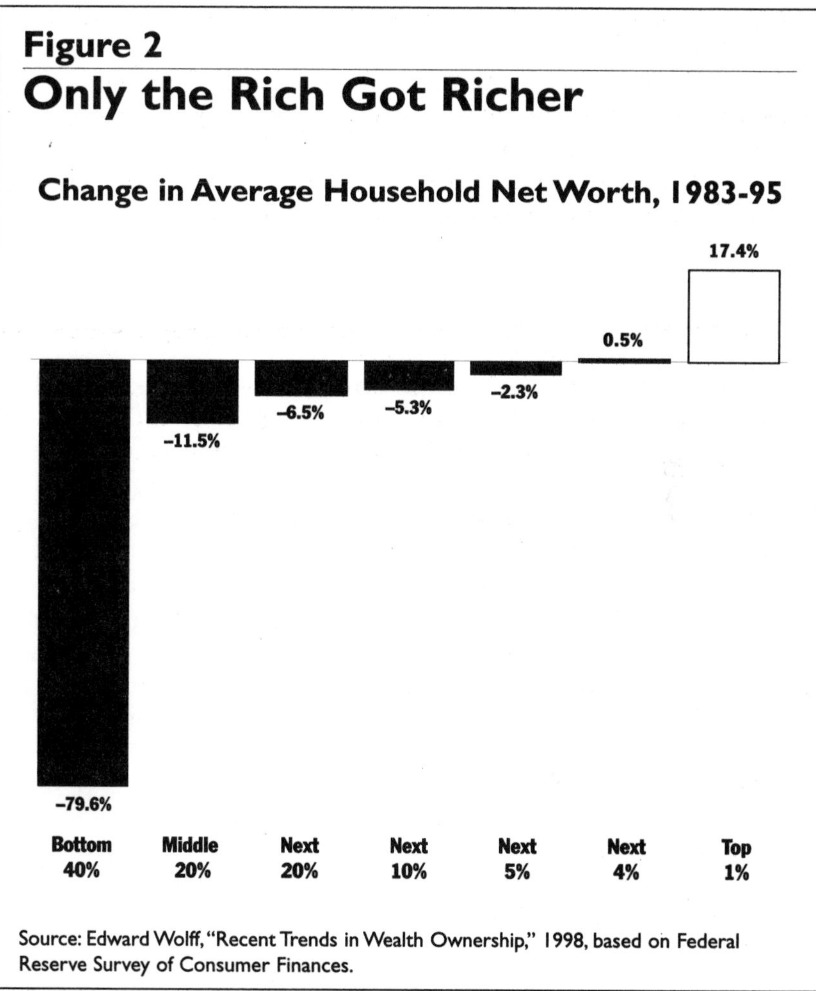

Source: Edward Wolff, "Recent Trends in Wealth Ownership," 1998, based on Federal Reserve Survey of Consumer Finances.

The percentage of households with zero or negative net worth (greater debts than assets) increased from 15.5 percent in 1983 to 18.5 percent in 1995—nearly one out of five households.[6] That's nearly double the rate in 1962, when the comparable figure was 9.8 percent—one out of ten households.[7]

Nine years into the longest peacetime expansion in U.S. history, average workers are still earning less, adjusting for inflation, than they did when Richard Nixon was president. No wonder many people have been working longer hours and going deeper into debt in an effort to keep up living standards and pay for college.

Many Americans can't make ends meet. Food banks and homeless shelters have been seeing more people with jobs at wages too low to support themselves and their families.

As we'll see later, we can reduce the wealth gap and strengthen national prosperity, if we have the will.

"It is a briefly amusing dinner-table game…to ask [affluent] people to guess how much money you'd need to be in the top 1 percent. 'Let's see, how low would you have to go,' mused a successful venture capitalist, revealing his certainty about his own rank. 'I'd say about $25 million. Answers vary widely, but not many guess low, and the median answer, in my unscientific study, is about $20 million. The correct answer is considerably less—between $2.5 and $3 million in net worth. As for income, according to the Internal Revenue Service, the top 1 percent of returns last year were those that listed adjusted gross incomes in excess of $200,000…

"The *Worth*-Roper Starch survey of the 1 percent found that 57 percent of respondents didn't consider themselves 'rich' (and only a quarter thought themselves 'upper class'), even though they have a median annual income of $330,000."

—Richard Todd, "Who Me, Rich?"
Worth, September 1997.

Table 1
What American Households Are Worth

Household Net Worth, 1995

Wealth Class	Average Net Worth	Range
Top 1%	$7,875,000	$2,419,000 and up
Next 4%	$1,115,000	$661,000 - $2,419,000
Next 5%	$471,700	$352,000 - $661,000
Next 10%	$246,800	$176,700 - $352,000
Fourth 20%	$116,800	$72,200 - $176,700
Middle 20%	$45,900	$23,300 - $72,200
Second 20%	$9,000	$190 - $23,300
Bottom 20%	–$7,100	up to $190

Source: Edward Wolff, based on the 1995 Federal Reserve Survey of Consumer Finances.

Figure 3
Wealth Concentration, Back to the Future

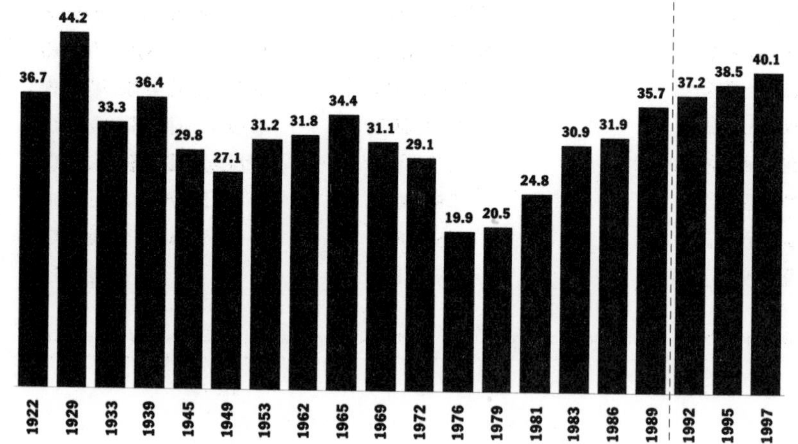

Source: Edward Wolff, *Top Heavy*, 1996, New Series Households data, pp. 78-79 (for years 1922-89) and "Recent Trends in Wealth Ownership," 1998 (for years 1992-97).

2

Stock Market Boom

The booming stock market has brought great wealth to some, but little or nothing to most Americans. At a 15 percent annual return—big by historical standards—investments double about every five years. The recent stock market has done much better than that.

Between 1983 and 1995, the Standard & Poor's 500 Index (S&P 500) delivered a huge cumulative return of 582 percent (with dividends reinvested). At the same time, the median household net worth dropped 11 percent. Median household net worth finally rose between 1995 and 1997, but it was still lower than the 1983 level. The stock market, meanwhile, grew more than 1,000 percent between 1983 and 1997.[8]

A thousand dollars invested in the stocks included in the S&P 500 Index in January 1983 would have grown to $11,175 by the end of 1997 (with dividends reinvested). This would have grown to $14,362 a year later. How about a million dollars? A million dollars invested by a wealthy American in 1983 would have grown to $11,175,000 by the end of 1997. This would have ballooned to $14,362,000 by the end of 1998. (See appendix for S&P 500 returns table.)

Despite the stories about delivery drivers getting rich off stocks traded online, the boom has bypassed most Americans. As of 1995 (the last completed Federal Reserve Survey of Consumer Finances), 40 percent of households owned stock directly and indirectly—including through a mutual fund, individual retirement account and defined contribution pension plan, for example. This is a significant increase from 32 percent in 1989, but still less than half of all households.[9]

A growing number of Americans own stock, but most still don't own much. Less than one-third of households (29 percent) owned stock worth more than $5,000 in 1995. Almost 90 percent of the value of all stocks and mutual funds owned by households was in the hands of the top 10 percent. Wealth projections through 1997 suggest that 86 percent of the benefits of the increase in the stock market between 1989 and 1997 went to the richest 10 percent of households, with 42 percent going to the top 1 percent alone.[10]

Figure 4
Who Benefited from the Stock Market Boom?

Distribution of Household Stock Market Gains, 1989-97, by Wealth Class

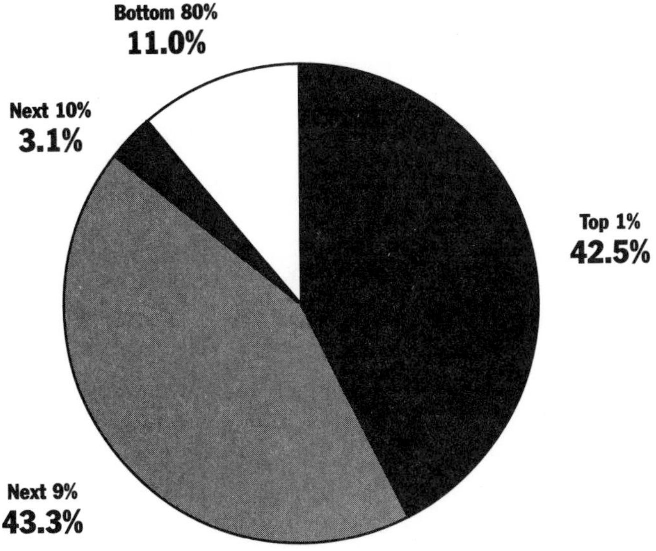

Source: Economic Policy Institute, based on Edward Wolff (1998), *The State of Working America 1998-99*, p. 271.

3

View From the Top

> "Not so long ago, a million dollars a year seemed like an absurdly extravagant income, and for nearly all the world's inhabitants, it is still the stuff of fairy tales. But in certain places in American business and finance—notably executive suites, Wall Street, and Silicon Valley—a million dollars a year today seems like... chump change."
>
> —*Fortune,* "Spoils of a Pig Market, September 7, 1998.

Between 1992 and 1995, the wealthiest 500,000 American households (in the top 1/2 percent) gained $1.6 trillion in assets, according to *Christian Science Monitor* reporter David Francis. Writing in 1997, he observed, "These super-prosperous families pocketed enough new wealth to write a check for the entire U.S. budget deficit and still cover the annual economic output of Italy...and then buy any company traded on the New York Stock Exchange—General Electric, for example."[11]

It took a net worth of at least $500 million to get on the *Forbes* 400 list of richest Americans in 1998—up from $475 million in 1997. The 1998 *Forbes* 400 had 189 billionaires—19 more than in 1997. Back in 1982, when *Forbes* inaugurated the 400, the price of individual admission was $91 million, and there were only 13 billionaires on the list. Among those high on the 1998 *Forbes* 400 are Microsoft multibillionaires Bill Gates, Paul Allen and Steven Ballmer, investment leader

Table 2
Buddy, Can You Spare a Billion?

The Richest Individuals and Families in the U.S., 1998

Name	Net Worth	Source
Bill Gates	$58.4 billion	Microsoft
Walton Family	$55.0 billion	Inheritance: Wal-Mart
Warren Buffett	$29.4 billion	Berkshire Hathaway
Paul Allen	$22.1 billion	Microsoft
Cox Family	$14.2 billion	Inheritance: Cox Enterprises
Michael Dell	$12.8 billion	Dell Computer
Steven Ballmer	$12.2 billion	Microsoft
Pritzker Family	$10.0 billion	Finance, Hotels, Manufacturing
John Kluge	$9.8 billion	Metromedia
Newhouse Family	$9.0 billion	Media Holdings

Source: *Forbes* 400, October 12, 1998. Net worth computed at stock market close on September 1, 1998.

Warren Buffet, Dell Computer founder Michael Dell and five heirs to the Wal-Mart fortune. Gates increased his net worth in 1998 by more than $2 million an hour.[12]

Forbes ran the numbers on the 400 richest Americans at the stock market close on September 1, 1998, when the Dow was still in a down at 7827 (the Dow ended the year back up at 9181). Still, the combined net worth of the *Forbes* 400 was $738 billion on September 1—way up from $624 billion in 1997. When the market closed on September 1, Microsoft stock, the engine of wealth for Bill Gates, the richest man on the *Forbes* 400, was at $101 per share and *Forbes* valued his total wealth at about $58 billion. A *Fortune* feature on Gates's finances (as of February 1999) listed Microsoft stock holdings of $76.5 billion plus an additional investment portfolio of $5 billion for a total of $81.5 billion—not including the $6.5 billion of assets in his family foundations.[13]

Table 3
What Billions Can Buy

Percentage of 1997-98 increase in net worth of *Forbes* 400 richest Americans ($114 Billion)	Extra Cost	Item
6.3%	$7.2 Billion	Double 1998 needs-based federal Pell Grants for college undergraduates
7.6%	$8.7 Billion	Head Start pre-school for the 2/3 of eligible children who aren't served.
13.2%	$15.1 Billion	Triple 1998 federal spending on training and employment
42.5%	$48.4 Billion	Cost to bring all poor Americans up to the official poverty line

1998 Budget Figures: Head Start: $4.35 billion. Pell Grants: $7.21 billion. Federal Spending on Training and Employment: $7.54 billion.

Sources: *Forbes* 400, October 12, 1998; *U.S. Statistical Abstract 1998,* Table 543, p. 342; U.S. Census Bureau, *Poverty in the United States: 1997* (September 1998), Table D, p. xii; Administration for Children and Families, U.S. Department of Health and Human Services, "Head Start 1998 Fact Sheet"; U.S. Department of Education, "FY 2000 Budget Summary," February 1999.

Bill Gates is a microcosm of the wealth gap. He has more wealth than the bottom 45 percent of American households combined.[14] By fall 1998, Gates ranked number five on the *American Heritage* list of the 40 richest Americans ever, right behind John D. Rockefeller, Andrew Carnegie, Cornelius Vanderbilt and John Jacob Astor.[15] At this writing, he's already passed Astor and well on his way to overtaking Vanderbilt.

In fall 1997, Bill Gates was worth more than the combined Gross National Product (GNP) of Central America: Guatemala, El Salvador, Costa Rica, Panama, Honduras, Nicaragua and Belize. By fall 1998, at about $60 billion, he

The Global Perspective

The United Nations Development Program's 1998 *Human Development Report* estimates that for the "developing" countries, "the additional cost of achieving and maintaining universal access to basic education for all, basic health care for all, reproductive health care for all women, adequate food for all and safe water and sanitation for all is roughly $40 billion a year. This is less than 4 percent of the combined wealth of the 225 richest people in the world." Bill Gates alone could lay the foundation with first-year funding and still have $40 billion or so left over.

According to the UN report, "The three richest people have assets that exceed the combined GDP [Gross Domestic Product] of the 48 least developed countries." Meanwhile, some 1.3 billion people still live on less than $1 a day and almost 3 billion live on less than $2 a day.

"In about 100 countries incomes today are lower in real terms than they were a decade or more ago," the UN report tells us. "In 70 countries with nearly a billion people consumption today is lower than it was 25 years ago." The average African household consumes 20 percent less today than it did 25 years ago.[16]

was worth more than the GNPs of Central America plus Jamaica and Bolivia. His early 1999 personal net worth of $81.5 billion is more than the combined GNP of Central America, Jamaica and Bolivia plus the Dominican Republic, Haiti and Grenada.[17]

Many rich Americans have been using their escalating wealth to splurge on luxuries. In his book, *Luxury Fever,* Robert Frank notes that spending on luxury goods grew by 21 percent from 1995 to 1996 while overall merchandise sales grew only 5 percent.[18]

Growing asset and income inequality has led to the development of a two-tier retail sector, one meeting the demand for luxuries and the other for the bargain shopper. As Jeff Gates observes in *The Ownership Solution,* retailers have adjusted to increased social polarization "by turning to a 'Tiffany/Kmart' marketing strategy that tailors their products and pitches to two very different Americas. Saatchi & Saatchi Advertising Worldwide warns its clients of 'a continuing erosion of our traditional mass market—the middle class,' while Paine Webber Inc. cautions investors to 'avoid companies that cater to the 'middle' of the consumer market.' In 1997, both

How To Quickly Spend a Million

"What's the best way to give a gift of 31 natural fancy yellow diamonds weighing a total of 69 carats? Fly on a chartered jet to Worth Avenue in Palm Beach, Fla., where you and that special someone can decide on the settings in person and stay in the Imperial Suite at the five-star Breakers hotel...The package also includes a morning at Spa Thira, a round of golf at the hotel course with a PGA pro, a shopping excursion on Worth Avenue, a limousine and driver on 24-hour call, and return trip via chartered jet." Price: $1,050,000.

—*Robb Report's 15th Annual Ultimate Gift Guide,* December 1998.

Kmart and Tiffany reported earning surges while the mid-scale chains such as J.C. Penney suffered."

Where are we headed? "The Atlanta-based Affluent Market Institute predicts that by 2005 America's millionaires will control 60 percent of the nation's purchasing dollars."[19]

In *Luxury Fever,* Robert Frank describes how the symbols of wealth and luxury in the eighties have been replaced by more extravagant versions—from fancier watches and custom-made suits to larger mansions and mega-yachts. He claims the reason is not because they add to human satisfaction or happiness, but because of social pressure. It's a kind of super-rich version of keeping up with the Dow Joneses. The unabashed "conspicuous consumption" economist Thorstein Veblen saw in the Gilded Age around the turn of the last century is back in vogue.

> "Any boob can buy a $100,000 wristwatch. If you really want the world to know you've arrived, you simply must find a peaceful, remote village, long populated by quiet old money [like the Hamptons and Martha's Vineyard], buy a nice old house, tear it down, and put up a blimp-hangar-sized mansion in its place."
>
> —*Fortune,* "Spoils of a Pig Market," September 7, 1998.

Frank highlights an "explosive growth in the construction of so-called trophy homes—mansions with more than 10,000 square feet of living space....Along one short stretch of the Florida coast near Palm Beach, 19 private residences ranging from 23,000 to 64,000 square feet have been built in the last several years; and in 1996 alone, 22 houses in the area exchanged hands in the market for prices above $10 million." Across the country in the Seattle area, Microsoft cofounder Paul Allen built a 74,000-square-foot house. The Allen compound "is approximately the same size as the build-

Figure 5
Economic Boom for Whom?

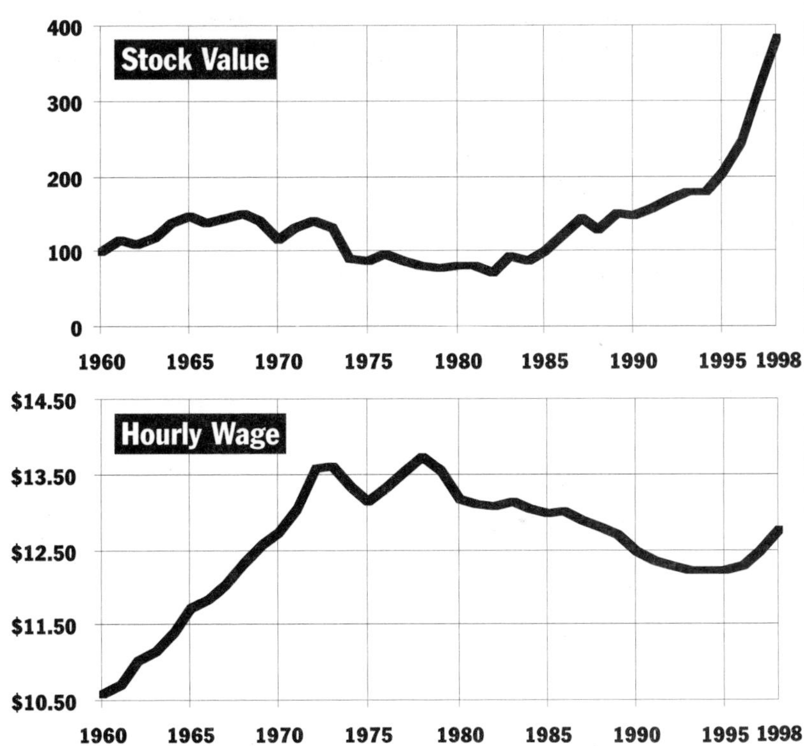

Stock Value: Standard & Poor's 500 Composite Index, adjusted for inflation, and indexed to 100 in 1960. This measure understates the total return because it covers stock prices only and does not assume that dividends are reinvested and compounded. See Appendix Table A-2 for compound returns.

Hourly Wages: For production and non-supervisory employees, adjusted for inflation (1998 dollars). Production and non-supervisory workers account for more than 80% of total wage and salary employment.

Source: Economic Policy Institute, 1999.

ing that houses Cornell's Johnson Graduate School of Management, in which roughly 100 faculty and administrative staff have offices and in which more than 600 students attend classes each day."[20]

Wealth imbalance comes into sharper relief during the holiday season. We hear a lot about shoppers splurging at upscale stores—and more families turning to food pantries and homeless shelters. Neiman Marcus has sold a $1,500 designer "Raj doll" replicating a "street urchin." It also sold an $850,000 belt for those who don't have to tighten them.[21]

4

The Shaky American Dream

A home. A rainy day cushion. Funds for retirement. Central to the American dream is this modest wealth—these assets that bring security to working families. Unfortunately, many Americans don't have them. At about $50,000, the total net worth of the median American household just about matches the projected sticker price of Ford's new supersized sports utility vehicle, the Excursion.

Many families don't have the security of enough assets to sustain them through periods of health crises or unemployment, much less lay the foundation for a comfortable retirement. In 1989, middle-income families with household heads between 25 and 54 had only enough financial wealth (net worth minus home equity) to sustain their current level of consumption for an average of 3.6 months; they could stretch that to 9 months by lowering their spending to 125 percent of the poverty line for a family of four. In 1995, middle-income families had even less: they had only enough financial wealth to last 1.2 months at their current level of consumption, or 1.8 months at 125 percent of the poverty line.[22]

While the middle class has seen their meager wealth erode, millions of other Americans don't have any wealth at all. They have zero or negative net worth. Negative net worth has long been accepted at certain stages of life, such as after buying a first home, before real equity has been built up. But it now appears that larger numbers of people are facing negative net worth at all stages of life, including the vulnerable

Table 4
Shrinking Nest Eggs

Family Financial Reserves, 1989 and 1995

Wealth class	Number of months that financial reserves can be used to sustain consumption: At current level	At 125% of the poverty standard for a family of 4
1989		
Top 20%	18.7	72.6
Fourth 20%	4.7	14.6
Middle 20%	3.6	9.0
Second 20%	0.7	1.0
Bottom 20%	0.0	0.0
1995		
Top 20%	19.0	61.3
Fourth 20%	3.5	7.9
Middle 20%	1.2	1.8
Second 20%	1.1	0.6
Bottom 20%	0.0	0.0

Source: Edward Wolff, "Recent Trends in Wealth Ownership," 1998, based on Federal Reserve Survey of Consumer Finances. Data for households with age of householder between 25 and 54. Financial reserves represent the median financial wealth (total net worth minus net equity in owner-occupied housing) for the respective quintiles.

Table 5
In the Red

Percentage of Households with Zero or Negative Net Worth or Financial Wealth, 1983-95

	1983	1989	1992	1995
Net Worth	15.5%	17.9%	18.0%	18.5%
Financial Wealth	25.7%	26.8%	28.2%	28.7%

Source: Edward Wolff, "Recent Trends in Wealth Ownership," 1998, based on Federal Reserve Survey of Consumer Finances. Financial wealth is net worth minus net equity in owner-occupied housing.

retirement years when assets are needed to replace earnings and supplement Social Security. By 1995, 18.5 percent of households had zero or negative net worth. That's nearly one out of five households.

The net worth of the poorest fifth of households averaged –$5,600 in 1997. That's down from –$3,000 in 1983.[23]

There are several components to the dismal asset picture for most Americans, among them long-term wage stagnation, pension erosion, decreasing access to affordable housing, diminished ability to save, rising debt and bankruptcy, and vanishing family farms.

5

The Wage Gap Underlies the Wealth Gap

Many Americans can't make ends meet today, much less build assets for the future. While the wealthy may worry about whether 1999 will see the end of the long-running bull market, workers are still trying to catch up with 1973. Despite long-overdue wage growth since 1996, hourly wages for average workers in 1998 were still 6.2 percent below 1973, adjusting for inflation; weekly wages were 12 percent lower than in 1973. Nonfarm business productivity grew nearly 33 percent in the same period.[24]

What if wages had kept rising with productivity? What if they were 33 percent higher in 1998 than they were in 1973? The average hourly wage in 1998 would have been $18.10, rather than $12.77. That's a difference of $5.33 an hour—more than $11,000 for a full-time, year-round worker. The 30 cents workers gained in their hourly wages between 1997 and 1998 pales by comparison.

The pace of recent wage growth has already slowed despite tight labor markets in many parts of the country.[25] The cumulative wages lost since 1973 will never be recovered—much less their lost investment potential.

The minimum wage has become a poverty wage. It was 19 percent lower in 1998 at $5.15 than it was in 1979, when it was worth $6.39, adjusted for inflation.[26] The minimum wage used to bring a family of three, with a full-time worker, above the official poverty line. Now it doesn't bring a full-time worker with one child above the official poverty line.[27]

Table 6
Lower Real Wages

Real Average Hourly and Weekly Earnings of Production and Nonsupervisory Workers, 1967-98

1998 dollars

Year	Hourly	Weekly
1967	$12.03	$457
1973	$13.61	$502
1979	$13.57	$484
1989	$12.70	$439
1992	$12.28	$422
1993	$12.22	$421
1994	$12.23	$424
1995	$12.23	$422
1996	$12.28	$422
1997	$12.47	$432
1998	$12.77	$442
% Change 1973-98	–6.2%	–12.0%

Between 1973 and 1998, productivity grew 32.8%.

Production and non-supervisory workers account for more than 80% of total wage and salary employment.

Source: Economic Policy Institute, 1999.

The share of workers earning low wages has been rising. Back in 1973, 23.5 percent of full-time, year-round workers did not earn enough to lift a family of four above the official poverty line. In 1997, 28.6 percent did not earn enough to do that.[28]

Looking at the poverty rates, you wouldn't know that the last recession officially ended in March 1991. In this, the world's richest nation, one out of five children live below the

Table 7

Poverty in the World's Richest Nation

Percentage of People in Poverty, 1997

	Under 50% of official poverty line	Under 100% of official poverty line	Under 150% of official poverty line*
All persons	5.4	13.3	22.5
under 18	9.0	19.9	30.6
under 6	10.1	21.6	33.4
Male	4.7	11.6	20.0
Female	6.1	14.9	24.8
White	4.3	11.0	19.7
under 18	6.6	16.1	26.3
Black	12.2	26.5	39.8
under 18	19.8	37.2	51.7
Hispanic	10.9	27.1	43.9
under 18	16.0	36.8	55.8

* Many analysts believe the official poverty line must be raised by at least 50 percent. The poverty thresholds for 1997 were set ridiculously low at $8,183 for one person, $11,062 for a 2-person family with one adult and one child under 18; $12,919 for a 3-person family with one child; and $16,276 for a 4-person family with two adults and two children.

Source: U.S. Bureau of the Census, *Poverty in the United States: 1997* (September 1998).

official poverty line. One out of seven children (14 percent) lived below the official poverty line in 1973, when the poverty measure was less divorced from reality than it is today.[29]

Young families, headed by persons under age 30, have been hit hard by falling wages and rising inequality. The poverty rate of two-parent young families more than doubled between 1973 and 1994. "If the fruits of economic growth had been shared equally among all families between 1973 and 1994," says the Children's Defense Fund, "then the median young family with children would have seen its income rise by 15 percent instead of falling by 33 percent," adjusting for inflation.[30]

These large shifts in the distribution of income significantly impact the distribution of wealth. If the poorest fifth of families had received the same share of after-tax income in 1994 as they did in 1977, they would have had $55 billion more in income. That's $55 billion in one year alone that could have gone not only to immediate needs, but to homeownership and investments for the future. The top 1 percent, on the other hand, would have had $146 billion less in income.[31] The money adds up. If an average top 1 percent family had invested their $132,955 share of 1994's $146 billion windfall in the S&P 500 at the end of that year, it would have grown to $384,771 by the end of 1998.[32]

Workers have been working longer hours in an effort to make ends meet. The average worker worked 1,868 hours in 1996, reports the Economic Policy Institute, compared with 1,823 in 1989 and 1,720 in 1973. The average worker worked 148 more hours in 1996 than their 1973 counterpart; that's equivalent to nearly four weeks longer.[33]

Between 1979 and 1997, middle-income families increased their annual hours of work by 315 hours (equivalent to nearly eight weeks of full-time work). If not for the extra paid work load of women, middle-income families would be far worse off. Unfortunately, women who work full time still earn only 74 cents for every dollar earned by men.

Just looking at the period between 1989 and 1997, annual work hours for middle-income families increased by 129 hours. While work hours increased 4 percent between 1989 and 1997, median family income (adjusting for inflation) grew only 0.6 percent, or $284, to reach $44,568. That additional $284 translates into $2.20 for every hour of extra work. In the same period, productivity went up 9.7 percent.[34]

Union jobs typically provide much better wages and benefits than nonunion ones. The median weekly wage of a full-time worker who belonged to a union in 1998 was $659, compared with $499 for those who did not. That's an annual

Table 8
Shifting Family Incomes

Change in After-Tax Income of Families, 1977-94

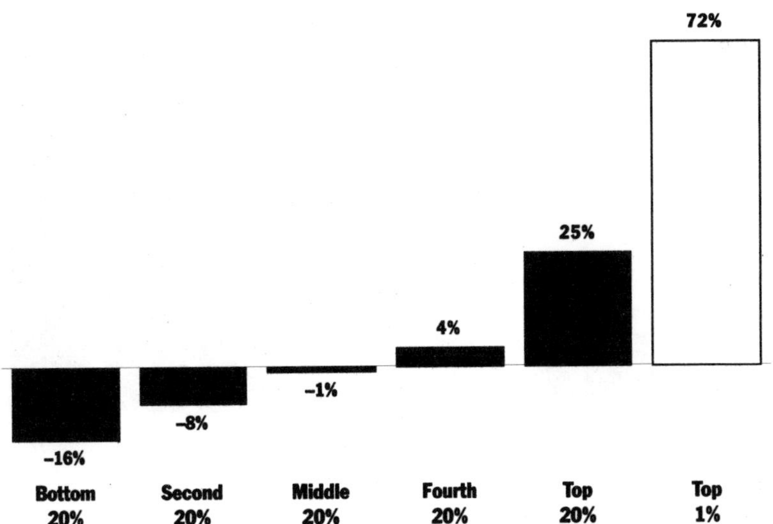

Average After-Tax Income in 1994

Income Class	Actual	If share of national income was the same as in 1977	The Difference
Bottom 20%	$7,175	$9,829	$2,654
Second 20%	$16,540	$19,352	$2,812
Middle 20%	$25,651	$27,448	$1,797
Fourth 20%	$37,226	$39,129	$1,903
Top 20%	$80,417	$71,736	– $8,681
Top 1%	$374,131	$241,176	– $132,955

Table reflects income after federal taxes. Because state and local taxes are even more regressive, the picture would show more inequality if they were included.

Source: Isaac Shapiro and Robert Greenstein, "Trends in the Distribution of After-Tax Income: An Analysis of Congressional Budget Office Data," Center on Budget and Policy Priorities, Washington, DC, August 14, 1997.

Figure 6
The Wage Gap

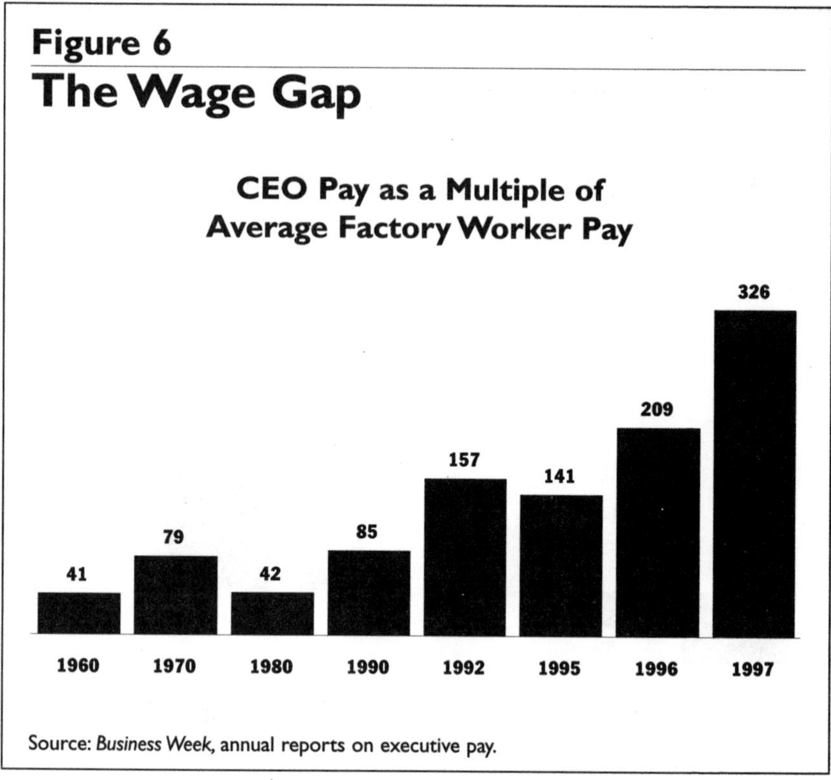

Source: *Business Week*, annual reports on executive pay.

wage differential of $8,320, not including better health, pension and other benefits paid to union members.[35]

But union jobs have been disappearing under the onslaught of downsizing, globalization and union busting. As *Business Week* put it in 1994, "Over the past dozen years, in fact, U.S. industry has conducted one of the most successful anti-union wars ever, illegally firing thousands of workers for exercising their right to organize."[36] Less than 14 percent of workers are union members now, down from 20 percent in 1983, 25 percent in 1973 and 35 percent in 1955.

Companies have been taking money from workers and giving it to executives. The average CEO in *Business Week's* annual survey made 326 times the pay of factory workers in 1997. That's way up from 1980, when CEOs made 42 times as much.

6

Eroding Pensions

Retired people's incomes have long been said to rest on a "three-legged stool" of Social Security (and Medicare), private savings and employer pensions. The stool is wobbling for some retirees and collapsing for others, as savings decline and pension coverage deteriorates.

Fewer than half of all workers (47 percent) were covered by pensions in 1996—down from 51 percent in 1979. To make matters worse, there has been a shift away from traditional "defined benefit" pension plans, which guarantee workers fixed retirement payments based on pre-retirement wages and years of service, toward "defined contribution" plans, such as 401(k)s, that take a chunk out of workers' paychecks and saddle employees with all the investment risk. Defined contribution plans accounted for 42 percent of all pension plans in 1997, up from 13 percent in 1975.[37]

Lower-wage workers are far less likely than high-wage workers to be covered by any employer-sponsored retirement plan, further exacerbating the wealth gap. Only 16 percent of the lowest wage workers (the bottom fifth by income) were covered by employer-provided pension plans in 1996, versus 73 percent of workers in the top fifth.[38] In addition to placing the investment risk on employees, defined contribution plans require employee contributions in order to receive company matching contributions, if offered. Many low-wage workers faced with the dilemma of choosing between feeding and housing their family today and saving for retirement in the

Figure 7
Reduced Pension Coverage

Percentage of Employees with Employer-Provided Pension Coverage, 1979-96

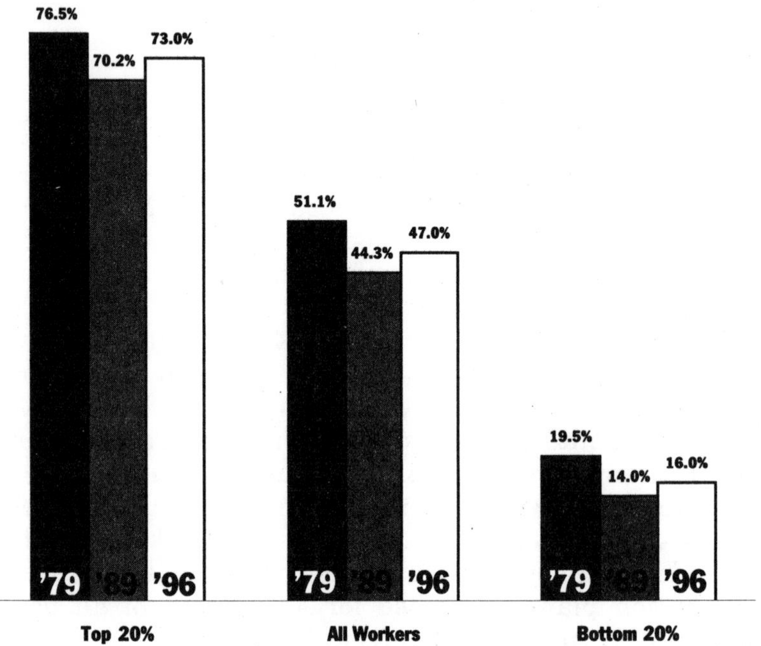

Source: Economic Policy Institute, *The State of Working America 1998-99*, p. 147. Figures cover private sector employees ages 18-64 who worked at least 20 hours a week and at least 26 weeks per year. Top and bottom 20% of workers are classified by wages.

future, do not participate in defined contribution plans even when given the option.

A 1997 *USA Today* study of 401(k) plans at the nation's 100 largest employers found that while 401(k) plans have become "Corporate America's most popular retirement benefit" and are rewarded through the tax code, they "are evolving

Aging Without Equity

Sharon* and her husband used to be homeowners, but no longer.

They both worked for years, he as a truck driver and she as a purchase order processor at Rockwell. By budgeting tightly, they saved enough to buy a small "starter house" in California and fix it up. "We thought our little home would be our security blanket for the future," says Sharon.

In 1993, both were laid off within two weeks of each other. Despite years of looking, neither has found a full-time job with decent pay and benefits. They have worked at part-time and temporary jobs that don't cover their basic bills. After their unemployment benefits and their savings ran out, they got behind on their mortgage and the bank repossessed their home. They moved into a rental house, and they fear eviction because they are sometimes behind on the rent. Their car recently broke down and they can't afford to fix or replace it.

A pension from Sharon's old Rockwell job pays them $200 a month, and they worry that small pension and Social Security will be their only retirement income. One of their part-time jobs offered an employer match for 401(k) contributions, but they couldn't afford to put anything in. At age 58, Sharon says, "There's no hope for us."

* Last name withheld to protect privacy.

into a largely upper-income benefit, turning out scores of 401(k) millionaires while potentially leaving many others without enough money to retire." The study found that "most of the best plans...are offered by manufacturers—high-paying companies with stable workforces, strong unions and a long tradition of generous pensions, now supplemented by 401(k) plans. Most of the worst...are in the retail and service industries, where pay is low...Those firms also are less likely to have [defined benefit] pensions."

USA Today found that the "workers least able to save for the future are further handicapped by 401(k) plans," which tend to have the lowest matching employer contributions, if any, a longer wait before eligibility and the strictest limits on how much employees can invest. The employment sectors with the poorest plans—retail and service—are the fastest growing ones. Moreover, "those jobs are dominated by women, who tend to outlive men and so rely longer on retirement income."[39]

7

Home $weet Home

As the Children's Defense Fund observes, "Homeownership has long been a central part of the American dream. It is also a major source of financial security and stability for young families, and an essential means of accumulating the equity that has enabled countless families later to borrow money in order to stave off a crisis, send a child to college, or help start a family business."[40]

With mortgage interest rates remaining at low levels, the U.S. homeownership rate hit a record 66 percent in 1998, but for people under age 55, the rates were actually lower in 1998 than in 1982.[41] The homeownership rate for people ages 30 to 34 was 53.6 percent in 1998, down from 57.1 percent in 1982. For those ages 35 to 39, it was 63.7 percent, down from 67.6 percent in 1982. For people ages 40 to 44, the homeownership rate was 70 percent in 1998, down from 73 percent and for those ages 45 to 49, it was 73.9 percent, down from 76 percent in 1982.[42]

The biggest government support for homeownership comes in the form of the tax deduction for mortgage interest on owner-occupied first and second homes. Unfortunately, much of the tax write-off goes to higher-income families. The more you can already afford to spend, the more the government subsidizes you. As the *New York Times* reports, for each dollar in tax savings from the mortgage-interest deduction "going to the average taxpayer making $200,000 or more, the average taxpayer in all lower income groups combined saves just 6 cents."[43]

For the fiscal year ending September 30, 1999, the mortgage deduction will add up to about $53.7 billion. That's $23 billion more than total 1998 federal spending by the Department of Housing and Urban Development (under $31 billion). The mortgage deduction costs 23 times as much as the credit for low-income housing investment ($2.3 billion).[44]

While tax subsidies for affluent homeowners remained high, federal funding for low-income housing was cut by 80 percent from 1978 to 1991, adjusting for inflation.[45] Not surprisingly, shortages of affordable housing have increased.

The Center on Budget and Policy Priorities reports that "in 1970, the number of low-cost rental units *exceeded* the number of low-income renters by 300,000. By 1995, there were only 6.1 million low-rent units for the nation's 10.5 million low-income renter households, a shortage of 4.4 million units."[46] Moreover, "Since housing assistance is not an entitlement, there are many more eligible families than there are families provided assistance, and waiting lists for housing assistance are very long in many areas. Census data indicate that there are 5.3 million unassisted families with 'worst case housing needs'; these are families that live in substandard housing or pay over half their income in rent."[47]

The affordable housing crisis is taking an increasing toll. On any given night, some 750,000 people are homeless; many more are the "hidden homeless," missed in varied counts. Over the course of a year, some 2 million people experience homelessness for some period of time. More than one-third of the homeless are families with children.[48]

In its 1998 survey of 30 major cities, the U.S. Conference of Mayors found that requests for emergency shelter by homeless families had risen 15 percent during the past year; 30 percent of the requests went unmet. The Mayors also found that more than one-fifth of the urban homeless were employed.[49] A 1998 survey of homeless people in Minnesota found that more than one-third are employed at least part-time and "the number of homeless people holding full-time jobs has more than doubled since 1991, to 17 percent."[50]

"Kenneth Lindo walks with bond traders and bankers through the gleaming lobbies of Wall Street during the day, his canvas messenger's bag heavy with checks and stock certificates from the longest bull market in memory. But at night he beds down at the 30th Street Men's Shelter in Manhattan, rolling his winter jacket in the sheet under his head.

"Until January, Mr. Lindo [age 44] had a pillow to call his own, in a Harlem room that cost $20 a day on his $5.50-an-hour pay—almost 70 percent of his take-home income."

—Nina Bernstein, "With a Job, Without a Home,"
New York Times, March 4, 1999.

8

Savings and the Cost of Living Squeeze

The U.S. personal savings rate has fallen from 8.6 percent in 1984 to 2.1 percent in 1997 and 0.5 percent in 1998.[51] The low savings rate is often used by conservatives as evidence of a character flaw in Americans who can't defer gratification. Researchers at the Federal Reserve Bank of Boston showed otherwise in a 1996 report, pointing to rising health care and other involuntary costs. Spending on durable goods such as cars, televisions and refrigerators held steady at 10 percent of disposable income, while spending on nondurables such as food, clothing and gasoline rose only slowly.[52]

People are spending larger portions of their income on health care, child care, housing and college tuition. Even the cost of saving itself is rising: there have been steep increases in bank service charges—especially for small accounts that can't meet the increasingly high minimums necessary to avoid fees.

A recent study by the Urban Institute found that many families with incomes up to 200 percent of the federal poverty level—which they call lower-income families—had trouble supporting themselves and their families. Nearly three in ten lower-income families were unable to pay the mortgage, rent or utility bills at some point in the prior year. Nearly half of lower-income families reported worrying about or having difficulty affording food.[53]

Low-income workers are turning increasingly to food banks, which, like homeless shelters, cannot keep up with the rising demand. In its 1998 survey, the U.S. Conference of

Mayors found that requests for emergency food increased an average of 14 percent during the past year. One out of five requests for food assistance went unmet.[54] The *American Journal of Public Health* reported in 1998 that 10 million Americans—including more than four million children—do not have enough to eat. The majority are in families with at least one employed person.[55]

A survey by Second Harvest, the nation's largest private network of food charities, found that nearly 40 percent of the households who received Second Harvest food in 1997 had at least one employed person. Recent visitors to a Greenwich, Connecticut food bank included "a cook from a local French restaurant, a construction worker, housekeepers from nearby estates who made the minimum wage, $5.15 an hour, and a woman who cared for the children of housekeepers."[56]

According to the Washington-based Wider Opportunities for Women and the Boston-based Women's Educational and Industrial Union, the self-sufficiency standard (the level of income necessary to meet all basic needs, including taxes) for an adult and preschooler in high-cost Boston is $32,279—nearly twice the official poverty line for a family of four. In lower-cost Berkshire County, Massachusetts it's $24,678.[57] No wonder many low-income workers—including growing numbers of former welfare recipients—can't make ends meet. Recent studies of former recipients and those combining work and welfare have found they typically earn between $8,000 and $10,800 annually. Most do not receive paid vacation, sick leave or health benefits from their employers.[58]

Unlike other industrialized nations, the United States does not provide universal health coverage. Reporting on the Census Bureau's latest health insurance data, *The New York Times* observed, "Despite the booming economy, the number of people without health insurance rose sharply last year, to 43.4 million, and the proportion of Americans lacking coverage reached the highest level in a decade, 16.1 percent." Employers are cutting back health coverage and "Medicaid rolls are down as stringent new laws prod people to move from welfare to work and the low-paying jobs they find often do not offer health benefits."[59]

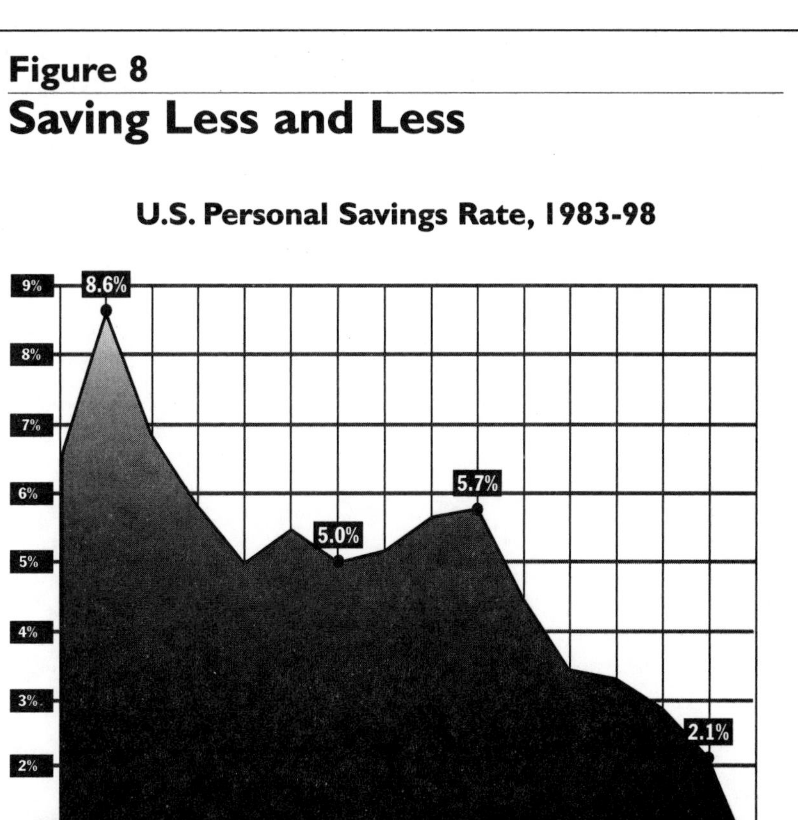

Source: U.S. Department of Commerce, Bureau of Economic Analysis. Figures are for personal savings as a percentage of disposable personal income.

According to a study by the Kaiser Family Foundation, in 1985, nearly two-thirds of all businesses with 100 or more employees paid the full cost of health care coverage. Only a third of the businesses did so a decade later. Many companies who do offer health benefits are deducting a growing share of the cost from workers' paychecks.[60] Lack of health insurance often means lack of health care or second-rate treatment and is associated with a 25 percent higher risk of death (adjusting for physical, economic and behavioral factors).[61] Members of Congress have publicly financed health care; everyone should.

9

The Debt Trap

American families have sunk deeper into debt. Household debt increased as real wages decreased. Debt as a percentage of personal income rose from 58 percent in 1973 to 76 percent in 1989 to an estimated 85 percent in 1997.[62]

The growth in household debt has helped keep the economy growing despite wage stagnation at home and economic turmoil abroad—at a significant cost to many families and the nation's long-term economic health. "The unsustainable growth in debt," says John Schmitt of the Economic Policy Institute, "undermines the stability of the recovery and threatens to magnify the impact of any downturn." A rise in interest rates "could put some newly-indebted households over the edge. Even a mild increase in unemployment could produce a substantial rise in bad debts, private bankruptcies and mortgage foreclosures."[63]

While much of the increased debt is due to rising costs while incomes have stagnated, some debt is driven by lenders' aggressive marketing and irresponsible loan practices. Households also may go deeper into debt to pursue the unaffordable high level of consumption that is promoted in our culture. We are bombarded by advertising that encourages us to meet every need—emotional, physical or spiritual—by buying material goods. Evidence abounds, however, that the cost-of-living squeeze and debt-pushing banks and corporations bear major responsibility for the rising level of household debt.

Figure 9

Deeper in Debt

Household Debt as a Percentage of Annual Personal Income, 1949-97

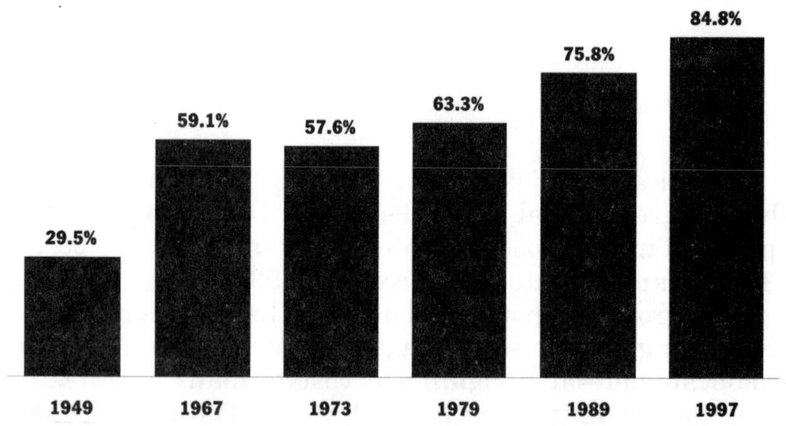

Source: Analysis of Federal Reserve Board data in Economic Policy Institute, *The State of Working America 1998-99*, p. 275. Figures for 1997 are preliminary.

Paying for College

A college degree is increasingly essential for decent earnings. During the 1980s and 1990s, as tuition costs skyrocketed, student financial aid came increasingly in the form of loans, not grants. The cost of attending a private college or university soared 146 percent in the 1980s, a higher rate than medical, home, food and car costs. But between 1980 and 1990, federal financial aid rose only 47 percent.[64] What about public colleges? As reported by *Business Week,* "Tuition at public colleges, where 80% of students go, jumped an inflation-adjusted 49% in the 1980s," but needs-based federal Pell grants trailed inflation by 13 percent.[65]

Mired in Debt

Julie Holmes is deep in debt. She owes money to a former landlord, to friends, family, her secretarial school and the phone company, and she has a couple thousand dollars in medical bills.

After secretarial school, Julie could find only temporary jobs. After so many temporary jobs, several employers rejected her for permanent positions because her job record looked unstable. Julie now lives in a homeless shelter in Oregon. She has severe medical problems that make it difficult for her to stand up or sit down for long periods of time. She keeps trying to get ahead, though, and recently got a job for 20 hours a week making $9.50 an hour.

She dreams of getting more education and running a business of her own someday, so she does not have to be burdened by debts that she cannot pay.

"Tuition and fees have risen 94% since 1989, nearly triple the 32.5% increase in inflation," reports *Business Week*.[66] In 1997, the average cost of one-year's tuition—not including thousands of dollars more in room and board—at a public four-year college was $3,321 (for in-state students); for a two-year college it was $1,283. The average annual tuition cost at a private four-year college was $16,531; it was $7,190 for a two-year college.[67]

Skyrocketing education costs have undermined progress for lower-income students. "Even as a good education has become the litmus test in the job market," said *Business Week* in 1994, "the widening wage chasm has made it harder for lower-income people to get to college. Kids from the top quarter have had no problem: 76% earn bachelor's degrees today, vs. 31% in 1980. But less than 4% of those in bottom-quarter families now finish college, vs. 6% then."[68]

> "If you were to announce that, given fiscal pressures, the door to social mobility that was good enough for the old generation is really no longer needed by the new one, you might as well stick a ticking bomb inside the social fabric of this country."
>
> —Barry Munitz, chancellor of the California State University System, 1997.[69]

Between 1990 and mid-1997, students borrowed at least $140 billion—more than total student borrowing over the prior three decades combined.[70] According to the Nellie Mae *National Student Loan Survey* (Nellie Mae, a subsidiary of the nonprofit Nellie Mae Foundation, is one of the nation's largest student loan providers), the median student had $13,000 in loans in 1997. Over one-quarter had used credit cards to help pay for tuition. Nearly all the respondents to Nellie Mae's survey also had non-education debt.[71]

Many survey respondents said that because of their student loan payments they had dropped out of undergraduate school, decided against graduate school or changed career plans, or delayed buying a house, purchasing a car or having children.[72] Forty percent of respondents said in 1997 that student loans caused them to delay buying a home, up from 25 percent of those surveyed in 1991; 31 percent said they had delayed purchasing a car, compared to 15 percent in 1991; 22 percent delayed having children, up from 12 percent in 1991.

In the Nellie Mae survey, students of color who did not complete a degree were more likely than white students to say that loans had prevented them from staying in school. About 70 percent of black, Hispanic and Asian/Pacific Islander borrowers gave this response compared to 43 percent of white borrowers. Half of the Pell grant recipients (Pell grants are only awarded to students with financial need) in the study said that their undergraduate debt had prevented them from attending graduate school, compared to 40 percent of the overall undergraduate population. In addition, 16 per-

The College Catch-22

In 1964, Jackie Hickerson's parents bought a home on an acre of land. Her mother was a homemaker. Her father, like most Americans, had not gone to college. With the modest income from her father's job as manager for a lumber company, her parents could also afford to send their children to a Catholic elementary school.

Today, one income is not enough for Jackie, a single mother, and her children. Jackie has long wanted to complete her bachelor's degree so she could get a decent job, but student loans and other college debt have held her back. The first time she went to college in the early 1980s, the Social Security survivor's benefits that covered part of her tuition were eliminated in federal budget cuts. She ended up with an unpaid tuition bill, thousands of dollars in student loans and no degree.

At times, Jackie worked two full-time minimum wage jobs to support her children and make her loan payments. Thanks to subsidized housing, which she was fortunate to get, and childcare help from family, Jackie was eventually able to get an associates degree at another college in 1994. Her 3.89 grade point average won her admission into Phi Beta Kappa and a scholarship to a four-year program for a bachelor's degree. But she couldn't accept the scholarship. The program required that she show all past transcripts, but her first college would not release her transcript until she completed her tuition payments. She was caught in a Catch-22. To make enough money to pay off her debt, she needed an education. To get an education, she needed to eliminate her debt.

Now 35, Jackie has finally finished paying off her tuition bill, although not her college loans. She qualifies for a Pell grant and has enrolled in environmental microbiology at the University of Vermont. Although she may be taking on more loans, she feels she has to risk digging the hole deeper if she is ever to get out at all.

cent of white, 19 percent of Latino and 26 percent of black borrowers had "strongly agreed" or "agreed" that they had significantly changed career plans because of their student debt.

The Debt Pushers: Credit Cards

In the 1990s, Americans began using credit cards more and paying off balances less. Credit-card debt as a percentage of household disposable income rose 60 percent from 1989 to 1997.[73]

Total credit card debt soared from $243 billion in 1990 to $560 billion in 1997.[74] Credit card limits have risen to the point that the average person can charge more than eight times what they already owe.[75] As of 1997, almost 60 percent of all American households carried credit card balances. The balances averaged more than $7,000, costing these households more than $1,000 per year in interest and fees.[76]

There is no mystery about why consumer debt skyrocketed when it did. As wages stagnated, banks and credit card companies began a huge and sometimes irresponsible marketing effort, flooding the country with easy credit. According to columnist Jane Bryant Quinn, "Credit card issuers mailed out 3.1 billion solicitations [in 1997]—30 for every American household. Where there's over-borrowing, lenders are equally to blame."[77]

Banks extend the bulk of all credit card debt. The Consumer Federation of America observes that "banks have been far less restrained in their marketing and credit extension than consumers have in their accumulation of credit card debt." While bank card debt rose 137 percent from 1992 to 1998, bank mailings rose 255 percent and unused credit lines rose 256 percent.[78] Banks have extended $2.4 trillion of card-related credit—$24,000 for each American household.[79]

Analyzing the financial services industry for investors, Standard & Poor's observed: "Financial services companies have been exceptionally active over the past few years in soliciting credit card accounts, and competition remains severe. These firms often entice consumers to open an account by offering a low annual financing rate for purchases or by waiving annual fees. Or they may offer low introductory rates for up to a year to customers who transfer balances from other credit card companies."[80] Borrowers who can't pay off their balances are then stuck when the rates rise after the introductory period, often to 17-21 percent or even higher.

Consumer lending is a very profitable business. As columnist Jane Bryant Quinn wrote in May 1998, "On average, credit cards are twice as profitable as all other banking activities... Lenders can make tons of money even with delinquencies at or near record levels, as they have been the last 12 months."[81] Banks collected the large majority of the $60 billion paid in interest and $10 billion paid in fees on credit cards in 1997.[82]

- MBNA is one of the country's largest lenders through bank credit cards with 21 million customers. Profits rose a spectacular 414 percent from 1990 to 1997, reaching $662.5 million in 1997. CEO Alfred Lerner got over $11 million in compensation that year.[83]

- American Express profits rose 96 percent from 1990 to 1997, to almost $2 billion. CEO Harvey Golub received an incredible 224 percent pay increase in 1997, including $27 million in stock option gains. His total compensation was $33.4 million in 1997, a year when American Express announced layoffs of 3,300 workers.[84]

- Household International, Inc. is the parent company of Household Financial Corporation, the nation's largest consumer finance company, offering credit cards, home equity and other secured loans. Household International's profits rose 192 percent from 1990 to 1997, to $686.6 million. CEO William Aldinger got $13.7 million in 1997 compensation, mostly in stock options.[85]

A disproportionate amount of the growth of credit card debt has occurred among lower-income Americans, those with annual incomes less than $25,000.[86] As of 1995, 27 percent of families with incomes less than $10,000 had credit card obligations that exceeded 40 percent of their incomes. Fewer than

5 percent of families earning more than $50,000 are burdened to that extent by credit card debt.[87]

Students are a special target of credit card companies. The U.S. Public Interest Research Group (PIRG) found that credit card companies target college students with aggressive marketing methods such as paying fees to campus groups to sponsor tables, gifts for those signing up for credit cards, initial "teaser" rates and misleading materials. The amount borrowed by students rose 11 percent in 1997, totaling over $38 billion.[88] Over two-thirds of undergraduates surveyed by Nellie Mae have credit cards.[89] About 14 percent of college students have balances of $3,000 to $7,000, and 10 percent owe more than $7,000.[90] Sixty-one percent of students surveyed by PIRG were responsible for their own bills.[91]

Rising Bankruptcy

Falling assets and rising debt have led to bankruptcy court for a record number of Americans. In 1998, 1.4 million individuals filed for personal bankruptcy, double the 718,000 who filed in 1990. While individual filings increased 3.6 percent from 1997 to 1998, business bankruptcy filings actually fell by 17 percent to about 44,000.[92]

The Standard & Poor's Industrial Survey of the financial services industry analyzed this trend for investors:

> Despite how well the economy has been performing, consumer bankruptcies continue to plague the industry, causing erratic charge-off levels. From an economic standpoint, the rise in bankruptcies is startling.
>
> Industry observers have attributed the alarming rise in bankruptcies to a number of factors. Some point to the ease with which consumers can now file for bankruptcy. Others pin the blame on financial services companies themselves, saying that lax underwriting standards have too easily let consumers outspend their financial resources. Credit card companies, in particular, have been chided by industry critics for making too much credit available to customers with marginal credit histories.

> From the consumer's point of view, any number of economic and societal factors could be to blame. Factors that could be pushing people to file for bankruptcy include: jobs lost to industry consolidation or workforce reductions; higher divorce rates; a greater percentage of the population in the 25-to-44 age bracket (for whom bankruptcy allegedly carries less of a stigma than for older generations); lack of financial discipline among many consumers; increased advertising by bankruptcy lawyers; and the widespread lack of health and automobile insurance, which sometimes allows a serious problem to wipe out an individual's financial resources.

Standard & Poor's proposed solution was the bankruptcy "reform" bill that passed the House, but not the Senate, in 1998.[93] The Consumers Union and the Consumers Federation of America both opposed the bill, which they said protected the interests of the credit industry while making it harder for families to get back on their feet. For example, credit card bills would have come before mortgage and car payments in the line for bankruptcy settlement payments, thus jeopardizing homes and jobs.[94]

Vanishing Family Farms

Historically, family farms were an important type of asset for low- and moderate-income families—one that provided a livelihood as well as a way of life passed down through generations. But family farms are disappearing. Since the 1980s, there has been a net decline of over 374,000 farmers.[95] Nebraska alone lost 12 percent of its family farmers and 34 percent of its rural population in the 1980s.[96] Farmers represent under 2 percent of the U.S. population, compared with 15 percent in 1950 and 40 percent at the turn of the century.[97]

Joel Greeno loves the independent lifestyle of dairy farming. He would much rather be working outside on his own farm than in a cramped factory. But Joel is the only farmer left in his family, and his independence comes at a high cost. Milk prices are very volatile, so there is no way to plan ahead, and the price of milk has not kept up with inflation.

Some multigenerational farm families are surviving a little better because they have the equity built up in previously paid-off land and equipment. Joel's parents were first generation farmers, and they went bankrupt. His brother had enough of the struggle and sold out.

When Joel started out, he bought a foreclosed farm that had been vandalized and gutted. Joel owes $78,000 for mortgage, equipment and cattle purchases. He spends approximately $972 a month servicing this debt. He tries to avoid more borrowing by repairing his old equipment and economizing in other ways.

Dairy farming is a very dangerous profession. Joel is constantly transporting heavy machinery and cattle. He does not have health insurance. He cannot afford it, but he also knows he really cannot afford *not* to have it in this profession where it is so easy to get hurt.

Joel feels a lot of stress wondering if he will make it. He also worries for the country as he watches large corporations swallow up agriculture and the small family farmer with it.

10

The Racial Wealth Gap

While the racial income gap is terribly wide, the racial wealth gap is even worse. According to Edward Wolff, the median black household had a net worth of just $7,400 in 1995—about 12 percent of the $61,000 in median wealth for whites. Median black financial wealth (net worth minus home equity) was just $200—a mere 1 percent of the $18,000 in median financial wealth for whites. In the same year, nearly one out of three black households had zero or negative net worth, twice the rate among whites.

Hispanic households have even less wealth than blacks. The median Hispanic household had a net worth of only $5,000 in 1995—just 8 percent of whites. Median financial wealth was actually zero—*nada.*[98]

Because of employment, housing, insurance and other discrimination, black and Latino families are far less likely than whites to own the homes in which they live. In 1995, the homeownership rate was 47 percent for blacks and 44 percent for Hispanics, about two-thirds the rate for white households (69 percent).[99] There has been some improvement in recent years, but there's still a long way to go.[100]

Back when the government was heavily involved in the housing business, the beneficiaries were mostly white Americans, giving them an unfair advantage in buying homes—an advantage that has reinforced the asset gap between whites and people of color to this day. Whites benefited directly by having higher rates of ownership and, indirectly, through the college educations, businesses and inheritances that home equity helped pay for.

The Federal Housing Administration (FHA) was created in 1934 to provide guaranteed mortgages for new construction. The GI Bill of 1944 provided Veterans Administration (VA) loan guarantees to subsidize home mortgages for returning veterans, almost all in heavily segregated suburbia. The FHA and VA programs insured about one-third of all homes purchased in the 1950s.[101]

"All through the 1930s and 1940s," explains political scientist Dennis Judd, "FHA administrators advised and sometimes required developers of residential projects to draw up restrictive covenants against nonwhites as a condition of obtaining FHA-insured financing." The U.S. Supreme Court ruled in 1948 that racial covenants could not be enforced, but *de facto* segregation continued. "Between 1946 and 1959, less than 2 percent of all the housing financed with the assistance of federal mortgage insurance was made available to blacks," writes Judd. "In 1960, not a single African-American could be counted among the 82,000 residents of Long Island's Levittown [New York]. The situation was typical."[102]

While blacks and other people of color were kept out of suburbia, they were "redlined" in the cities, again with serious impact on their ability to accumulate wealth through home equity. A 1968 National Commission on Urban Problems deplored the "tacit agreement among all groups—lending institutions, fire insurance companies, and FHA"—to redline inner city neighborhoods, denying them credit and insurance.[103]

Housing discrimination has remained a problem in the 1990s. For example, according to a 1991 Department of Housing and Urban Development (HUD) report of fair housing testing audits in 25 U.S. cities, blacks encountered discrimination more than half of the time.[104]

A 1991 Federal Reserve Board study, analyzing 1990 Home Mortgage Disclosure Act (HMDA) data, found racial lending disparities across the country, with blacks and Latinos rejected twice as often as white applicants, regardless of income. A crucial 1992 report by the Boston Federal Reserve that systematically controlled for the largest range of

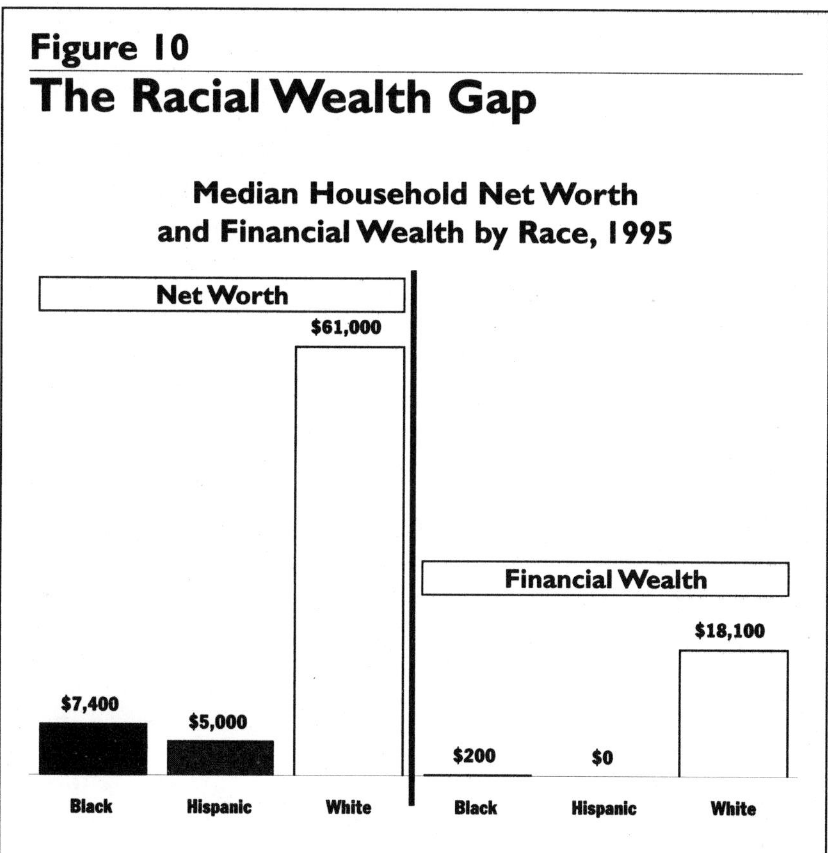

Source: Edward Wolff, "Recent Trends in Wealth Ownership," 1998, based on Federal Reserve Survey of Consumer Finances. Financial wealth is net worth minus net equity in owner-occupied housing.

financial, employment and other lending variables confirmed the widespread bias the banks had kept trying to rationalize away. The report found that blacks and Latinos "were two to three times as likely to be denied mortgage loans as whites. In fact, high-income minorities in Boston were more likely to be turned down than low-income whites."[105]

In 1999, the *Kansas City Star* analyzed mortgage applications taken by more than 500 area banks and mortgage companies from 1992 to 1997. As reported by Ted Sickinger, a former commercial loan officer, "lenders still reject minority mortgage applicants far more frequently than they do whites. Even high-income minorities are rejected more frequently than whites with lower incomes."

Moreover, "most loans made in minority neighborhoods refinance existing debt and are made by companies that often charge higher interest rates and fees. In white neighborhoods, by contrast, most loans are made at market rates and go to buy homes—the kind of lending that helps borrowers build wealth."

Unlike the overt redlining of the past, the *Kansas City Star* found "discrimination with a smile." In the words of HUD Secretary Andrew Cuomo, "Housing discrimination is much more insidious today than it was two or three decades ago."[106]

Making matters worse, some of the same banks denying conventional mortgages and home-improvement loans in predominantly black and Latino neighborhoods have colluded with con-artist contractors who provide financing for repair work at sky high interest rates of 24, even 40 percent. Second mortgages have been taken out with or without the homeowners' approval—using tactics such as hiding second mortgage agreements in a stack of contracts and loan documents or even forging signatures. Many of those intentionally targeted were elderly homeowners with paid-off mortgages, vulnerable to equity theft. To keep their homes, owners then had to pay the extortionist loans even when, as often the case, the repair work was shoddy or never completed. Many foreclosures have resulted.

Some of the banks benefiting from the loan-sharking cited their purchase of second mortgages in minority communities as evidence they were fulfilling the mandates of the Community Reinvestment Act.[107] Unfortunately, loan scams are just one of the ways low-income communities ending up paying literally or proportionately more than higher-income communities for banking, credit, housing, insurance, transportation, food, health care and other goods and services.[108]

Melvin Oliver and Thomas Shapiro analyzed the asset gap in their book, *Black Wealth / White Wealth*. Even if differences in income, occupation, education and other factors are

> "Homeownership, propelled by that first mortgage, is still the foundation of the American Dream.
>
> "The keys to one's own home unlock a series of economic doors, including access to better schools, better jobs and safer neighborhoods.
>
> "Equity in a home can secure a business loan, lead to a more comfortable retirement, or help pay for a child's education or home purchase.
>
> "The benefits multiply across families, neighborhoods and generations.
>
> "Or not."
>
> —Ted Sickinger,
> "When the door is blocked to buying a home,"
> *Kansas City Star,* February 28, 1999.

removed from the equation, a difference of $43,143 in average net worth remained in 1988. They call it "the costs of being black." For married couples, the difference was greater: $46,294.[109] Housing discrimination is a major factor. Inheritance is another. White parents generally have far greater resources to pay for their children's college education, help them with their first home purchase and bequeath them assets at death.

As Oliver and Shapiro observe, "Wealth signifies the command over financial resources that a family has accumulated over its lifetime along with those resources that have been inherited across generations."[110]

Inequality is a Health Hazard for Rich and Poor

Inequality is a matter of life and death—and not just for the poor. In the words of health experts, "the greater the income differences within populations (whether of whole countries or of cities or larger administrative areas within countries), the worse their health. This helps explain why the United States, the richest and most powerful country in the world (spending more than any other on health care), ranks below 25th in the league of countries ordered by life expectancy. Income differences between rich and poor are bigger in the United States than in any other developed nation."[111]

A recent report in the *American Journal of Public Health* found that higher income inequality is associated with increased mortality at all per capita income levels. "Given the mortality burden associated with income inequality," the report concludes, "business, private, and public sector initiatives to reduce economic inequalities should be a high priority."[112]

Recommendations to Reduce the Wealth Gap

> "Issues of equity and social cohesion [are] issues that affect the very temperament of the country. We are forced to face the question of whether we will be able to go forward together as a unified society with a confident outlook or as a society of diverse economic groups suspicious of both the future and each other."
>
> —William McDonough, chair,
> Federal Reserve Bank of New York.[113]

Increased inequality is not the result of natural phenomena like sun spots or shifting winds. It is the result of over two decades of public policies and private corporate practices that have benefited asset owners at the expense of wage earners.

In the words of *Business Week* reporters William Wolman and Anne Colamosca, there has been a "triumph of capital and a betrayal of work."[114] The economic winners are those who own substantial assets—much more than just a home, a car and some savings. The economic losers are people whose security is linked to a paycheck or government safety-net income.

Tax policy, trade policy, government spending and regulation have all been tilted in favor of affluent asset owners. Other nations have experienced technological change and global competition without dramatic increases in inequality. Here, wealth and political influence closely entwine to shape policies that favor those at the top.

In Edward Wolff's words, "Wealth, more so than income, directly translates into political power."[115] People with wealth are not only influencing policy in their favor through campaign contributions and lobbying, they are making policy. More than one-third of U.S. senators are millionaires.

Asset-building policies have been an integral part of U.S. history, from the Homestead Act in the 19th century to the mid-20th century GI Bill that allowed millions of Americans to have debt-free college educations to current homeownership and retirement subsidies through the tax code.

Unfortunately, the government generously subsidizes those who don't need any help with building assets. An estimated $125 billion in federal subsidies are directed to corporations in the form of tax loopholes, direct cash transfers and subsidized access to public resources.[116] This misdirected "corporate welfare" benefits large corporations and affluent individuals. Government assistance should be focused on non-affluent households, small businesses, family farms and democratic enterprises such as cooperatives.

"Money makes money," said Adam Smith, author of *The Wealth of Nations,* long ago. Immediate reforms are needed to enable low- and moderate-income families to earn, save and invest more money and build asset security.

Thoughtful Americans are advancing a variety of proposals that would narrow the wealth gap. They range from Jeff Gates's proposals to expand ownership to Rep. Martin Sabo's legislation linking the tax deductibility of executive salaries to the wages paid their employees to Senator Robert Kerrey's proposal for asset accounts at birth. What follows is a brief survey of some of these initiatives.

Asset-Building Policies

KidSave Accounts Act. Legislation advanced by Senator Robert Kerrey (D-NE) with bipartisan support would guarantee every American child $1,000 at birth, plus $500 a year for children ages one to five, to be invested until retirement. Through compound returns over time, the account would grow substantially, provide a significant supplement to Social Security and other retirement funds, and enable many more Americans to leave inheritances to their children. That would strengthen opportunities and asset-building across generations. KidSave would be administered under Social Security; parents and then the grown children would have the option of allocating the funds among high- medium- and low-risk funds (similar to the Thrift Savings Plan available to federal employees). At an 8.5 percent return, for example, $1,000 set aside at birth would be worth $250,000 at age 65; the additional $2,500 set aside in the child's first five years would be worth $470,000.[117]

"Under our proposal, every baby in America would enter life owning a piece of their country," says Kerrey. "The result isn't just more retirement security. It's also an opportunity to transform an 'us-vs.-them' economy—in which good news for the wealthy often seems to be bad news for everyone else—to a 'we're all in this together' economy."[118]

Broadening Employee Ownership. While the overall trend in wealth growth has been toward concentration, a significant exception is among employee owners. As of 1997, more than 8 percent of total corporate equity was owned by nonmanagement employees, up from less than 2 percent in 1987. This ownership takes the forms of Employee Stock Ownership Plans (ESOPs), profit-sharing plans, widely granted stock options and other forms of broad ownership. In 1997, average employee owners had about $35,000 in corporate equity above what they were able to save from their paychecks.[119]

In *The Ownership Solution,* Jeff Gates urges us to look beyond wage and job policies to expand the ownership stake that workers and their communities have in private enterprise. There are a range of public policies that could promote broader ownership and reward companies that share the wealth with employees, consumers and other stakeholders. These include encouraging employee ownership through government purchasing, licensing rights, public pension plan investments, loans and loan guarantee programs and so on.[120]

Individual Development Accounts (IDAs). IDAs are like individual retirement accounts, but are targeted to low- and moderate-income households to assist them in asset accumulation. Participants in IDAs may have their contributions matched by public or private dollars. A number of private charities have financed pilot IDA programs through community-based organizations. A generous federally funded matching IDA program would provide significant opportunities for asset-poor households to build wealth.[121] Participants could withdraw funds from IDAs in order to purchase a home, finance a small business or invest in education or job-training. Even small amounts of money can make a substantial difference in whether or not individuals get on the asset-building train.

USA Accounts. In his January 1999 State of the Union address, President Clinton introduced a new version of individual retirement accounts called Universal Savings Accounts. The proposal is short on specifics, but the basic idea is to invest 11 percent of the budget surplus to match the contributions of low- and moderate-income workers in private accounts.[122]

Living Wages and Full Employment. People would obviously have greater ability to save if their wages were higher. Low real wages have pushed a growing number of families into debt. Decent wages would enable families to save money, purchase assets and plan for the future. Wage remedies include higher state and federal minimum wages and the passage of living wage ordinances. Protecting the right of employees to organize and join unions also greatly increases their wage earning potential. Laws prohibiting employment discrimination on the basis of race, gender and so on should be strongly enforced.

Of course, you can't earn wages if you can't find a job. Government policies should promote full employment and assure jobs for every American who needs one.

Expand Earned Income Credit and Raise No-Tax Threshold. Progressive tax policies can enable families to keep more money in their pockets. These include an expanded earned income credit, an increased personal exemption and a higher no-tax threshold.

Dedicated Tax Exempt Savings Programs. A politically popular way of promoting savings and asset-building is through Individual Retirement Accounts, which exempt accounts from taxation at the front end or, like the Roth IRA, from the back end. Similar accounts have been proposed to enable people to save for homeownership. The tax credit for college education went into effect this year. Over the long run, we should make sure that tax policies encourage access to higher education and asset-building by low- and middle-income Americans rather than disproportionately subsidize wealthier Americans.

Affordable Housing. Owning a home has long been considered a stepping stone to building assets. Public policies that increase access to homeownership include subsidized mortgages and mortgage insurance, downpayment assistance funds, second mortgage subsidy programs, and grants and low-interest loans for home improvements and weatherization. Stricter enforcement of fair housing and community reinvestment laws would remove barriers to asset-building for people of color.

Homeownership is not the only tenure option that should be promoted, however, as it is not appropriate for all households at all stages of life. Nor should homeownership be considered the only "asset account" for low- and moderate-income families, as it has its risks. Access to decent and very affordable cooperative and rental housing would enable many people to save and meet other financial security goals. Public subsidies should be targeted to "third sector" housing ownership including community land trusts, housing cooperatives, mutual housing and other models that reduce housing costs and preserve long-term affordability.

Policies Addressing the Overconcentration of Wealth

Many of the proposals described above are aimed at assisting people with very little savings and assets to increase their personal net worth. We believe, however, that there will continue to be distortions in who benefits from public policy unless we address the issue of the overconcentration of wealth and power at the very pinnacle of the population.

While there is some consensus that government should play a role in helping the assetless build a nest egg, there are strongly divergent views as to how to appropriately address the overconcentration of assets at the top. Here are some initiatives to consider:

Income Equity Act. Presently, businesses can deduct executive salaries from corporate taxes as a "reasonable business" expense. In 1993, reformers passed legislation to cap the deductibility of salaries at $1 million. But there are significant loopholes such as allowing high salaries if they are deemed "salary for performance." Companies routinely call their executive salaries "performance-based" so that taxpayers continue subsidizing exorbitant compensation.

Rep. Martin Sabo (D-MN) has introduced legislation to cap the tax deductibility of all salaries and bonuses at 25 times the lowest-paid worker in a firm. Companies could still pay whatever salaries or bonuses they chose, but the legislation would provide an incentive to increase salaries at the bottom. In the 105th Congress, there were over 60 cosponsors for this bipartisan legislation.

Taxing Capital Gains Like Wages. The tax burden is being shifted off of large asset owners and onto wage earners. The Social Security payroll tax has taken an increasingly bigger bite out of the paychecks of most wage earners, especially low- and middle-wage earners since income subject to Social Security tax is capped (the cap is now $72,600). Meanwhile, taxes on capital gains have been reduced substantially. A fair tax system would not favor income from assets over income from wages.

Because of the 1997 Taxpayer Relief Act, which gave relief to the rich by reducing the tax rate on long-term capital gains from 28 percent to 20 percent, many workers now pay a higher tax rate on income from wages than wealthy investors pay on realized capital gains. Billionaire investor Warren Buffet was troubled by this gross inequality. At the 1997 annual meeting of his company, Berkshire Hathaway, he said, "The capital gains tax rate is just about right. I don't think it's appropriate...to have me taxed at 28 percent if I sell my Berkshire shares when someone who's trying to find a cure for cancer is taxed at 39 percent."

Conservatives in Congress are proposing to further reduce the capital gains rate from 20 percent to 15 percent. This proposal would cost the U.S. Treasury approximately $15.5 billion a year in tax revenues, with three-quarters of the benefits of the tax cut going to households with more than $200,000 in income.[123] By contrast, the "10 percent" tax plan advanced by House Minority Leader Richard Gephardt (D-MO) taxes all types of income at the same rate, whether from wages, capital gains, dividends or interest. The plan raises the no-tax threshold and has progressive tax rates starting at 10 percent—the rate most Americans would pay.

Maintain Strong Estate and Inheritance Taxes. Government policies should facilitate the transfer of family assets from one generation to the next. But we should also be concerned about excessive wealth transfers and their distorting impact on the economy, democracy and culture. At very high levels, particularly in households in the top 1/2 percent, the transfer of wealth represents a transfer of power, which reinforces economic and political inequality.

Only a small share of households pay estate taxes today because only estates over $625,000 at the time of death are subject to the tax (the threshold is being raised incrementally to $1 million), and there are safeguards for family farms and family-owned businesses. With planning, married couples can already pass $1.2 million to their heirs estate-tax free. Estate taxes should not be reduced, much less repealed, as some propose.

Wealth Taxation. The overconcentration of wealth and power presents such a significant challenge that wealth taxation should be considered. European countries with wealth taxes include Austria, Denmark, Finland, Germany, Luxembourg, the Netherlands, Norway, Spain, Sweden and Switzerland. With the exception of Spain, most of these wealth taxes have been in place for at least 60 years. While there are no direct wealth taxes in the United States, wealth is subject to estate taxes and taxes on capital gains.

Edward Wolff proposes a wealth tax in *Top Heavy* (based on the Swiss model) with progressive tax rates, the highest of which is well under 1 percent (0.03 percent). Most households would fall entirely below the wealth tax threshold.[124] While it would be challenging to agree on an appropriate form of wealth taxation for the United States, a more significant challenge may be constitutional. The original 16th Amendment establishing the income tax may not provide the constitutional authority for a wealth tax.

Looking Forward

The wealth gap poses serious consequences for our economy, our democracy and our civic life. Too large a concentration of wealth and power distorts our economic institutions and undermines our self-governing democracy. Even if the pace of wealth inequality slows, the current level of inequality fosters a perilous polarization of our nation.

The wealth gap reinforces (and is reinforced by) widening disparities in education, economic opportunity and quality of life. Even the affluent lose from inequality as it hurts life expectancy for rich and poor, fuels violence and denies all of us the contributions of people whose opportunities are denied.

We have highlighted initiatives that would reduce the wealth gap, energize our society and strengthen our people, economy and democracy for the long run. It's time we did so. We owe it to all the heirs of the America we leave behind.

Resources

To find out more information or get involved in activities to narrow the wealth gap, contact:

United for a Fair Economy
37 Temple Place, 2nd floor, Boston, MA 02111
Phone (617) 423-2148, Fax (617) 423-0191
E-mail stw@stw.org

Additional copies of *Shifting Fortunes* are available for $6.95 each plus $1.00 postage and handling per book. Bulk discounts are available.
To order, call toll free (877) 564-6833.

United for a Fair Economy membership dues are $25.00 a year. *The Fair Economy Organizing Kit* is available for $5.00.

Responsible Wealth, a project of United for a Fair Economy
Responsible Wealth is a network of businesspeople, investors and affluent individuals in the top 5 percent of income and assets who are concerned about growing economic inequality and are taking action to promote a fair economy.
Phone (617) 423-2148, Fax (617) 423-0191
E-mail rw@stw.org

Visit United for a Fair Economy and Responsible Wealth on the web at www.stw.org.

Further Reading

Ann Crittenden, *Killing the Sacred Cows: Bold Ideas for a New Economy* (New York: Penguin, 1993).

G. William Domhoff, *Who Rules America? Power and Politics in the Year 2000* (Mountain View, CA: Mayfield Publishing Company, 1998).

Nancy Folbre, with the Center for Popular Economics, National Priorities Project and United for a Fair Economy, *The Field Guide to the U.S. Economy,* revised edition (New York: The New Press, forthcoming fall 1999).

Robert Frank, *Luxury Fever: Why Money Fails to Satisfy In an Era of Excess* (New York: Free Press, 1999).

James K. Galbraith, *Created Unequal: The Crisis in American Pay* (New York: Free Press/Century Fund, 1998).

Jeff Gates, *The Ownership Solution: Towards a Shared Capitalism for the 21st Century* (Reading, MA: Addison Wesley, 1998).

Frank Levy, *The New Dollars and Dreams: American Incomes and Economic Change* (New York: Russell Sage Foundation, 1998).

Peter Medoff and Holly Sklar, *Streets of Hope: The Fall and Rise of an Urban Neighborhood* (Boston: South End Press, 1994).

Lawrence Mishel, Jared Bernstein and John Schmitt, Economic Policy Institute, *The State of Working America 1998-99* (Ithaca: Cornell University Press, 1999).

Melvin L. Oliver and Thomas M. Shapiro, *Black Wealth / White Wealth: A New Perspective on Racial Inequality* (New York: Routledge, 1995).

Robert Pollin and Stephanie Luce, *The Living Wage: Building a Fair Economy* (New York: New Press, 1998).

Juliet B. Schor, *The Overspent American: Upscaling, Downshifting, and the New Consumer* (New York: Basic Books, 1998).

John E. Schwarz and Thomas J. Volgy, *The Forgotten Americans: Thirty Million Working Poor in the Land of Opportunity* (New York: W.W. Norton, 1992).

Michael Sherraden and Neil Gilbert, *Assets and the Poor: A New American Welfare Policy* (Armonk, NY: M.E. Sharpe, 1991).

Holly Sklar, *Chaos or Community? Seeking Solutions, Not Scapegoats for Bad Economics* (Boston: South End Press, 1995).

Edward N. Wolff, "Recent Trends in Wealth Ownership," a paper for the Conference on Benefits and Mechanisms for Spreading Asset Ownership in the United States, New York University, December 10-12, 1998, forthcoming in a reader edited by Thomas Shapiro and Edward N. Wolff.

Edward N. Wolff, *Top Heavy: The Increasing Inequality of Wealth in America and What Can Be Done about It* (New York: New Press, 1996).

William Wolman and Anne Colamosca, *The Judas Economy: The Triumph of Capital and the Betrayal of Work* (Reading, MA: Addison-Wesley Publishing, 1997).

Glossary

Asset: Anything owned that has value such as cash, stocks, a home or other real estate. Examples of **financial assets** include cash, savings accounts, stocks, mutual funds, bonds, IRAs, etc.

Mean: The average value. If you add up the net worth of all the households in the United States and divide by the total number of households, you will get the mean net worth.

Median: The middle value. If you took all the households in the United States and lined them up in order of their net worth, Bill Gates's household would be at one end, the poorest household in the country would be at the other end, and the household in the middle of that line would have the median net worth.

Net Worth: Assets minus debts (liabilities). In other words, what you own minus what you owe. If you have $1,000 in the bank, $10,000 in an IRA, but still owe $100,000 in mortgage payments on a home valued at $150,000, and have a college loan balance of $10,000, you would have a net worth of –$51,000. (See footnote 2 in the text for a more detailed explanation of net worth as defined in the Edward Wolff data cited in this report).

Pension Plan: A pension plan is designed to give a worker a monthly income after he or she retires. Social Security is a type of public pension plan, funded through payroll taxes. A little less than one-half of all workers also have employer-provided pension plans:

- **A defined-benefit pension** guarantees a certain amount of money per month to the retiree, based on pre-retirement wages and years of service.
- **A defined-contribution pension** plan, such as a 401(k) plan, relies on paycheck contributions, which employers may supplement, and places all the risk with the employee. If the investments in the employee's 401(k) plan lose money, the employee is out of luck.

Profits: A company's earnings minus expenses, such as the cost of labor, raw materials, equipment, advertising, etc.

Quintile: One fifth, or 20 percent, of the population.

Real Wages: The value of wages, adjusted for inflation. This way, wages in different years may be more appropriately compared.

Stock Options: Commonly seen in the pay packages of corporate executives, a stock option is the right to purchase shares of company stock at a pre-set price. For example, if you were an executive, you might receive an option to buy 20,000 shares of your company's stock at $50 a share. When the price of that stock hits $100 a share, you might decide to exercise your option and buy the stock from your company at $50, then immediately sell it on the open market at $100 a share, for a $50-a-share profit, netting you $1 million before taxes. What if the stock price falls and the options are "underwater," worth less than the pre-set price? Companies often re-price existing stock options so that they cost less than the current stock price, guaranteeing the executive a profit.

Appendix

Table A-1

Distribution of Household Net Worth, Financial Wealth and Income, 1982-97

	Percentage Share of Wealth or Income Held by						
Year	Top 1%	Next 4%	Next 5%	Next 10%	Next 20%	Middle 20%	Bottom 40%
A. Net Worth							
1983	33.8	22.3	12.1	13.1	12.6	5.2	0.9
1989	37.4	21.6	11.6	13.0	12.3	4.8	– 0.7
1992	37.2	22.8	11.8	12.0	11.5	4.4	0.4
1995	38.5	21.8	11.5	12.1	11.4	4.5	0.2
1997	40.1	21.9	11.2	11.4	10.7	4.4	0.5
B. Financial Wealth							
1983	42.9	25.1	12.3	11.0	7.9	1.7	– 0.9
1989	46.9	23.9	11.6	10.9	7.4	1.7	– 2.4
1992	45.6	25.0	11.5	10.2	7.3	1.5	– 1.1
1995	47.2	24.6	11.2	10.1	6.9	1.4	– 1.3
1997	48.6	23.6	10.7	8.9	6.4	2.1	– 0.3
C. Income							
1982	12.8	13.3	10.3	15.5	21.6	14.1	12.3
1988	16.6	13.3	10.4	15.2	20.6	13.2	10.7
1991	15.7	14.8	10.6	15.3	20.4	12.8	10.5
1994	14.4	14.5	10.4	15.9	20.6	13.6	10.7

Source: Edward Wolff, "Recent Trends in Wealth Ownership," 1998. Figures for 1997 projected from the Federal Reserve Survey of Consumer Finances on the basis of change in asset prices between 1995 and 1997. Financial wealth is net worth minus net equity in owner-occupied housing.

Table A-2

Cumulative and Annualized Return on the S & P 500 Stock Index, 1970-98

Period	Cumulative Return	Annualized Return
Jan. 1, 1995 - Dec. 31, 1998	189.4%	30.4%
Jan. 1, 1989 - Dec. 31, 1998	477.1%	19.1%
Jan. 1, 1983 - Dec. 31, 1998	1336.2%	18.1%
Jan. 1, 1983 - Dec. 31, 1997	1017.5%	17.4%
Jan. 1, 1980 - Dec. 31, 1998	2099.2%	17.7%
Jan. 1, 1973 - Dec. 31, 1998	2649.8%	13.6%
Jan. 1, 1973 - Dec. 31, 1997	2039.6%	13.0%
Jan. 1, 1970 - Dec. 31, 1998	3781.4%	13.4%

Source: Bloomberg L.P., Standard & Poor's 500. Index is capitalization weighted with dividends reinvested. Annualized figures are derived from compounded quarterly returns.

Table A-3

Average Values of Household Net Worth, Financial Wealth and Income, 1982-95

In thousands (1995 dollars)

Year	Top 1%	Next 4%	Next 5%	Next 10%	Next 20%	Middle 20%	Bottom 40%	All
Net Worth								
1983	6,708	1,110	482.6	260.6	124.9	51.9	4.4	198.8
1995	7,875	1,115	471.7	246.8	116.8	45.9	0.9	204.5
% Change	17.4	0.5	– 2.3	– 5.3	– 6.5	– 11.5	– 79.6	2.9
Financial Wealth								
1983	6,187	906	354.0	158.7	57.0	12.3	– 6.3	144.2
1995	7,400	963	352.2	158.5	54.0	11.3	–10.6	156.9
% Change	19.6	6.4	– 0.5	– 0.1	– 5.3	– 7.8	– 68.3	8.8
Income								
1982	563.5	145.6	90.4	67.9	47.5	31.1	27.1	43.9
1994	625.0	157.4	90.5	69.2	44.7	29.7	23.3	43.5
% Change	10.9	8.1	0.0	2.0	– 5.8	– 4.5	– 14.0	– 0.8

Source: Edward Wolff, "Recent Trends in Wealth Ownership," 1998, based on Federal Reserve Survey of Consumer Finances. Financial wealth is net worth minus net equity in owner-occupied housing.

Table A-4

Median and Average Household Net Worth, Financial Wealth and Income, 1983-97

1995 dollars

	Net Worth		Financial Wealth		Income	
Year	Median	Average	Median	Average	Median	Average
1983	$51,100	$198,800	$11,000	$144,200	$31,000	$43,900
1989	$54,600	$227,700	$13,000	$170,000	$29,600	$45,800
1992	$46,600	$221,400	$10,900	$168,800	$28,300	$46,500
1995	$45,600	$204,500	$10,000	$156,900	$30,000	$43,500
1997	$49,900	$226,400	$11,700	$176,200		
% Change						
1989-95	−16.5	−10.2	−23.1	−7.7	+1.4	−5.0
1989-97	−8.6	−0.1	−10.0	+3.6		
1983-95	−10.8	+2.9	−9.1	+8.8	−3.2	−0.9
1983-97	−2.3	+13.9	+6.4	+22.2		

Source: Edward Wolff, "Recent Trends in Wealth Ownership," 1998. Figures for 1997 projected from the Federal Reserve Survey of Consumer Finances on the basis of change in asset prices between 1995 and 1997. Financial wealth is net worth minus net equity in owner-occupied housing.

Table A-5

Household Net Worth and Financial Wealth by Race and Ethnicity, 1983-95

1995 dollars

	1983	1989	1992	1995
Average Net Worth				
Black	$43,700	$46,100	$49,400	$40,800
Hispanic	$37,800	$45,200	$59,100	$51,300
White	$232,300	$274,800	$265,900	$242,400
Black as a % of White	19%	17%	19%	17%
Hispanic as a % of White	16%	16%	22%	21%
Median Net Worth				
Black	$4,400	$2,000	$11,200	$7,400
Hispanic	$2,600	$1,700	$4,000	$5,000
White	$66,900	$79,400	$66,600	$61,000
Black as a % of White	7%	3%	17%	12%
Hispanic as a % of White	4%	2%	6%	8%
Average Financial Wealth				
Black	$22,000	$22,500	$28,200	$21,200
Hispanic	$11,200	$22,100	$38,000	$29,300
White	$171,100	$207,700	$204,700	$188,400
Black as a % of White	13%	11%	14%	11%
Hispanic as a % of White	7%	11%	19%	16%
Median Financial Wealth				
Black	$0	$0	$100	$200
Hispanic	$0	$0	$0	$0
White	$18,600	$25,100	$20,500	$18,100
Black as a % of White	0%	0%	1%	1%
Hispanic as a % of White	0%	0%	0%	0%

Source: Edward Wolff, "Recent Trends in Wealth Ownership," 1998, based on Federal Reserve Survey of Consumer Finances. Financial wealth is net worth minus net equity in owner-occupied housing.

Table A-6

Percentage of Households With Zero or Negative Net Worth by Race and Ethnicity, 1983-95

Based on average net worth

	1983	1989	1992	1995
Black	34.1	40.7	31.5	31.3
Hispanic	40.3	39.9	41.2	38.3
White	11.3	12.1	13.8	15.0
Black Zero-or-Negative Net Worth Rate as a % of White	301	338	228	209
Hispanic Zero-or-Negative Net Worth Rate as a % of White	355	331	298	256

Source: Edward Wolff, "Recent Trends in Wealth Ownership," 1998, based on Federal Reserve Survey of Consumer Finances.

Table A-7

Household Income by Race and Ethnicity, 1982-94

1995 dollars

	1982	1988	1991	1994
Average Income				
Black	$25,700	$23,200	$26,000	$23,000
Hispanic	$28,800	$23,800	$24,500	$30,900
White	$47,700	$52,200	$51,900	$47,700
Black as a % of White	54%	45%	50%	48%
Hispanic as a % of White	60%	46%	47%	65%
Median Income				
Black	$18,700	$13,200	$18,100	$17,000
Hispanic	$22,200	$16,700	$17,000	$22,000
White	$33,500	$34,800	$32,000	$32,000
Black as a % of White	56%	38%	57%	53%
Hispanic as a % of White	66%	48%	53%	69%

Source: Edward Wolff, "Recent Trends in Wealth Ownership," 1998, based on Federal Reserve Survey of Consumer Finances.

Table A-8

Homeownership by Race and Ethnicity, 1983-95

1995 dollars

	1983	1989	1992	1995
Black	44.3%	41.7%	48.5%	46.8%
Hispanic	32.6%	39.8%	43.1%	44.4%
White	68.1%	69.3%	69.0%	69.4%
Black Homeownership Rate as a % of White	65%	60%	70%	67%
Hispanic Homeownership Rate as a % of White	48%	57%	62%	64%

Source: Edward Wolff, "Recent Trends in Wealth Ownership," 1998, based on Federal Reserve Survey of Consumer Finances.

Notes

1. Bloomberg L.P., Standard & Poor's. Return using capitalization weighted S&P 500 index, with dividends reinvested.

2. Edward N. Wolff, "Recent Trends in Wealth Ownership," a paper for the Conference on Benefits and Mechanisms for Spreading Asset Ownership in the United States, New York University, December 10-12, 1998, Table 2, "The Size Distribution of Wealth and Income, 1983-1997." Wolff's computations are based on the Federal Reserve Surveys of Consumer Finances, 1983, 1989, 1992, 1995. The 1998 Survey will be available in late 1999. Wolff's 1997 figures are "projected on the basis of Board of Governors of the Federal Reserve System (1998), Flow of Funds accounts. Projections are based on the average change in total asset and liability values between the last quarter of 1995 and the last quarter of 1997, standardized for the change in the CPI and the change in the number of households in the U.S. Projections of the median are based on the wealth composition of the middle wealth quintile in 1995."

   Wolff's net worth figures represent the current value of all marketable or fungible assets less the current value of debts. Fungible assets include assets that can be readily converted to cash (e.g., owner-occupied housing and other real estate; cash, savings and certificates of deposit; stocks, mutual funds, bonds and other financial securities; the cash surrender value of life insurance plans, IRAs, 401 (k) plans; etc.). Consumer durables such as automobiles, furniture and so on are excluded "since these items are not easily marketed or their resale value typically far understates the value of their consumption services to the household."

   For historical data and trends see Edward N. Wolff, *Top Heavy: The Increasing Inequality of Wealth in America and What Can Be Done about It* (New York: New Press, 1996).

3. Edward Wolff cited in "A Scholar Who Concentrates...on Concentrations of Wealth," *Too Much,* Winter 1999, p. 8.

4. Wolff, "Recent Trends in Wealth Ownership," Table 2, "The Size Distribution of Wealth and Income, 1983-1997."
5. *Ibid.,* Table 1, "Mean and Median Wealth and Income, 1983-1997." As Wolff notes, "Financial wealth is a more 'liquid' concept than marketable wealth, since one's home is difficult to convert into cash in the short term"; pp. 6-7.
6. *Ibid.,* Table 1, "Mean and Median Wealth and Income, 1983-1997."
7. Ferdinand Lundberg, *The Rich and the Super-Rich* (New York: Lyle Stuart, 1968), citing Federal Reserve "Survey of Financial Characteristics of Consumers," 1962.
8. Bloomberg L.P., Standard & Poor's. Return using capitalization weighted S&P 500 index, with dividends reinvested.
9. Lawrence Mishel, Jared Bernstein and John Schmitt, Economic Policy Institute, *The State of Working America 1998-99* (Ithaca: Cornell University Press, 1999), p. 267.
10. *Ibid.,* pp. 260, 266-73. Also see Aaron Bernstein, "A sinking tide does not lower all boats," *Business Week,* September 14, 1998.
11. David R. Francis, "Where did all the money go? Not far," *Christian Science Monitor,* July 16, 1997.
12. *Forbes* 400, October 12, 1998; *Forbes* 400, September 13, 1982. The *Forbes* 400 is available on the *Forbes* website (www.forbes.com).
13. Andy Serwer, "How Bill Gates invests his money," *Fortune,* March 15, 1999.
14. Edward Wolff cited in "A Scholar Who Concentrates."
15. "The American Heritage 40," *American Heritage, October 1998.*
16. United Nations Development Program, *Human Development Report 1998* (New York: Oxford University Press, 1998), pp. 2, 7, 30, 37, 51.
17. GNP data from the World Bank, 1997 figures (latest available).
18. Robert Frank, *Luxury Fever* (New York: Free Press, 1999), pp. 18-19, citing Rebecca Piirto Heath, "Life on Easy Street," *American Demographics,* April 1997, p. 38.
19. Jeff Gates, *The Ownership Solution: Towards a Shared Capitalism for the 21st Century* (Reading, MA: Addison Wesley, 1998), p. 6.
20. Frank, *Luxury Fever,* pp. 21-22.
21. Neiman Marcus 1997 Christmas catalog. Also see *Robb Report Annual Ultimate Gift Guide for the Affluent Lifestyle.*
22. Wolff, "Recent Trends in Wealth Ownership", Table 10, "Accumulated Financial Reserves of Families by Income Quintile In Terms of Number of Months Reserves Can Sustain Consumption, 1983-1995."
23. Data provided by Edward Wolff, 1998.

24. Data provided by the Economic Policy Institute, March 1999. Also see *The State of Working America 1998-99,* pp. 127, 153-55.

25. Economic Policy Institute, *Jobs Fax,* January 8, 1999 and March 5, 1999. Also see U.S. Department of Labor, Bureau of Labor Statistics, *Employment and Earnings,* January 1999.

26. Data provided by the Economic Policy Institute, March 1999. The minimum wage was raised to $4.75 in 1996 and $5.15 in 1997.

27. A full-time, year-round worker earning the minimum wage of $5.15 would make $10,712 for 52 weeks. The official 1998 poverty thresholds (the latest available) were $8,480 for one person, $11,235 for an adult and child, $12,750 for a three-person family and $16,813 for a four-person family. U.S. Census Bureau, "Poverty Thresholds: 1998," February 3, 1999.

28. Economic Policy Institute, "Economic Snapshots: Working full time fails families," February 10, 1999, on website (www.epinet.org).

29. For discussion of the outdated poverty measure, see, for example, Holly Sklar, *Chaos or Community? Seeking Solutions, Not Scapegoats for Bad Economics* (Boston: South End Press, 1995), pp. 11-14 and Economic Policy Institute, *The State of Working America 1998-99,* pp. 283-88.

30. Arloc Sherman, *Rescuing the American Dream: Halting the Economic Freefall of Today's Young Families with Children* (Washington, DC: Children's Defense Fund, 1997), p. 13.

31. Isaac Shapiro and Robert Greenstein, "Trends in the Distribution of After-Tax Income: An Analysis of Congressional Budget Office Data," Center on Budget and Policy Priorities, Washington, DC, August 14, 1997.

32. Assumes investment in the S&P 500 with index dividends reinvested. Cumulative return for January 1, 1995 through December 31, 1998 was 189.4 percent.

33. Economic Policy Institute, *The State of Working America 1998-99,* pp. 122-23.

34. Economic Policy Institute, "Wage gains, more hours lift family income above pre-recession level," September 25, 1998.

35. U.S. Department of Labor, Bureau of Labor Statistics, *Employment and Earnings,* January 1999, p. 220.

36. *Business Week,* May 23, 1994.

37. Economic Policy Institute, *State of Working America 1998-99,* pp. 147-48.

38. *Ibid.,* p. 147.

39. Anne Willette, "Exposing the 401(k) Gap," *USA Today,* November 24, 1997. Also see Anne Willette, "Taking a closer look at your 401(k),"

USA Today, November 24, 1997 and editorial, "401(k)s help workers save but don't go far enough, *USA Today,* November 25, 1997.

40. Sherman, *Rescuing the American Dream,* p. 35.

41. U.S. Census Bureau, Table: "Homeownership Rates for the United States, by Age of Householder and by Family Status: 1982 to 1998," revised February 3, 1999, on website (www.census.gov). *U.S. Statistical Abstract 1998,* Table 1215, p. 726.

42. *Ibid.*

43. David Cay Johnston, "Mortgage Tax Break: Who Gets What," *New York Times,* January 10, 1999.

44. *U.S. Statistical Abstract 1998,* Table 544, p. 343. Also see Citizens for Tax Justice, *The Hidden Entitlements,* 1996.

45. Lynn A. Curtis and Vesta Kimble, *Investing in Children and Youth, Reconstructing Our Cities* (Washington, DC: The Milton S. Eisenhower Foundation, 1993), p. 14.

46. Jennifer Daskal, *In Search of Shelter: The Growing Shortage of Affordable Rental Housing,* Center on Budget and Policy Priorities, June 15, 1998.

47. Barbara Sard and Jennifer Daskal, "Housing and Welfare Reform: Some Background Information," Center on Budget and Policy Priorities, July 16, 1998.

48. National Alliance to End Homelessness, "Facts about Homelessness," website (www.naeh.org); National Coalition for the Homeless, "How Many People Experience Homelessness," NCH Fact Sheet #2, February 1999 and "Who is Homeless?" NCH Fact Sheet #3, February 1999, website (www.nch.ari.net); National Law Center on Homelessness and Poverty, website (www.nlchp.org).

49. U.S. Conference of Mayors, "Summary: A Status Report on Hunger and Homelessness in American Cities—1998," website (www.usmayors.org).

50. Mark Brunswick, "For the working homeless, day begins and ends at shelter," Minneapolis *Star Tribune,* February 26, 1999.

51. U.S. Department of Commerce, Bureau of Economic Analysis. In 1998, the Commerce Department began using a narrower definition of income that magnified the savings rate decrease.

52. Gordon Matthews, "Drop in Savings Rate Isn't for Lack of Trying," *American Banker,* November 12, 1996. This article summarizes the report by Federal Reserve analysts Lynn Elaine Browne and Joshua Gleason: "The Saving Mystery, Or Where Did the Money Go?" *New England Economic Review,* September-October 1996.

53. Urban Institute, *Snapshots of America's Families, The National Survey of America's Families,* January 1999.

54. U.S. Conference of Mayors, "Summary: A Status Report on Hunger and Homelessness in American Cities—1998."

55. Sandra G. Boodman, "Researchers Put Number on U.S. Hunger," *Washington Post,* March 31, 1998.

56. Andrew C. Revkin, "Welfare Policies Alter the Face of Food Lines," *New York Times,* February 26, 1999. Also see Revkin, "As Need for Food Grows, Donations Steadily Drop," *New York Times,* February 27, 1999 and Project Bread and the Center on Hunger and Poverty at Tufts University, *Hidden Hunger, Fragile Futures,* 1998.

57. Diana Pearce and Jennifer Brooks with Laura Henze Russell, *The Self-Sufficiency Standard for Massachusetts* (Washington, DC: Wider Opportunities for Women, September 1998). Also see, Barbara Ehrenreich, "Nickel-and-Dimed: On (Not) Getting By in America," *Harpers,* January 1999; John E. Schwarz, "The Hidden Side of the Clinton Economy," *Atlantic Monthly,* October 1998; John E. Schwarz and Thomas J. Volgy, *The Forgotten Americans: Thirty Million Working Poor in the Land of Opportunity* (New York: W.W. Norton, 1992).

58. Sharon Parrot, *Welfare Recipients Who Find Jobs,* Center on Budget and Policy Priorities, November 16, 1998. Also see Children's Defense Fund and the National Coalition for the Homeless, *Welfare to What? Early Findings on Family Hardship and Well-Being,* 1998.

59. Robert Pear, "Americans Lacking Health Insurance Put at 16 Percent," *New York Times,* September 26, 1998.

60. Peter T. Kilborn, "Uninsured in U.S. Span Many Groups," *New York Times,* February 26, 1999.

61. Linda J. Blumberg and David W. Liska, *The Uninsured in the United States: A Status Report* (Washington, DC: Urban Institute, April 1996) and Spencer Rich, "For Those with Modest Incomes, Health Insurance Bill is Little Help," *Washington Post,* May 3, 1996. Also see Dennis P. Andrulis, "Access to Care is the Centerpiece in the Elimination of Socioeconomic Disparities in Health," *Annals of Internal Medicine,* September 1, 1998 and Roni Rabin, "Queens Health: Taking a Risk Living Without a Safety Net: Insurance a Key to Healthy Lives, but Many Have None," *Newsday,* November 15, 1998.

62. Economic Policy Institute, *The State of Working America 1998-99,* pp. 274-75. Because of lower interest rates, debt service as a percentage of disposable income has gone up less.

63. John Schmitt, "What Has the Dow Done for you Lately?" Economic Policy Institute Viewpoints, February 18, 1999, on website (www.epinet.org).

64. Mary Jordan, *Washington Post,* "Panel to call for new student-aid system," *Boston Globe,* February 3, 1993; Associated Press, "US college costs still rising faster than income," *Boston Globe,* September 22, 1993.

65.“Inequality: How the Gap Between Rich and Poor Hurts the Economy,” *Business Week,* August 15, 1994, p. 79.

66.Meg Lundstrom, “Intro to Haggling,” *Business Week,* March 15, 1999, p. 104.

67.*U.S. Statistical Abstract 1998,* Table 312, p. 195. The maximum award for the 1999 Pell Grant is $3,125, with an average award of $1,935 for the 3.8 million recipients. See U.S. Department of Education, “FY 2000 Budget Summary,” February 1999, on department website (www.ed.gov).

68.“Inequality: How the Gap Between Rich and Poor Hurts the Economy,” *Business Week,* August 15, 1994, p. 79.

69.Quoted in Peter Applebome, “Rising Cost of College Imperils Nation, Report Says,” *New York Times,* June 18, 1997, which summarized the findings of the Commission on National Investment in Higher Education report, “Breaking the Social Contract: The Fiscal Crisis in Higher Education.” The Commission was convened by the Council for Aid to Education, an independent subsidiary of the Rand Corporation.

70.Joshua Wolf Shenk, “In Debt All the Way up to Their Nose Rings,” *US News & World Report,* June 9, 1997, p. 38.

71.Nellie Mae, “Life After Debt: Results of the National Student Loan Survey,” 1998. The sample surveyed was composed of 65 percent undergraduates and 35 percent graduate students, all Nellie Mae borrowers, from across the United States. The survey was done in 1997.

72.*Ibid.,* p. iv.

73.Frank, *Luxury Fever,* p. 46, citing *Business Wire,* “Credit Card Debt Reaches All-Time High Among Lower-Income Americans,” March 24, 1997.

74.*U.S. Statistical Abstract 1998,* Table 822, p. 523.

75.Standard & Poor’s, “Industry Surveys—Financial Services: Diversified,” August 27, 1998, p. 2.

76.Stephen Brobeck, The Consumer Federation of America, “Recent Trends in Bank Credit Card Marketing and Indebtedness,” July 1998.

77.Jane Bryant Quinn, “How credit card issuers fuel over-borrowing,” *Washington Post,* May 17, 1998.

78.Brobeck, “Recent Trends in Bank Credit Card Marketing and Indebtedness,” p.3.

79.Consumer Federation of America, “Card Issuers Hike Fees and Rates to Bolster Profits,” press release, November 5, 1998, p. 2.

80.Standard & Poor’s, “Industry Surveys—Financial Services: Diversified,” August 27, 1998, p.7. Also see, Robert D. Hershey Jr., “Sales of Credit Card Accounts are Hurting Many Consumers,” *New York Times,* March 2, 1999.

81. Quinn, "How credit card issuers fuel over-borrowing."

82. Brobeck, "Recent Trends in Bank Credit Card Marketing and Indebtedness," p. 4.

83. Value Line Publishing, December 4, 1998; MBNA 1998 Proxy Statement filed with the Securities and Exchange Commission.

84. Value Line Publishing, December 4, 1998; United for a Fair Economy, *Executive Excess: 1998,* based on American Express 1998 Proxy Statement filed with the Securities and Exchange Commission and layoff data from Challenger, Gray & Christmas surveys.

85. Value Line Publishing, December 4, 1998; Household International 1998 Proxy Statement filed with Securities and Exchange Commission.

86. Frank, *Luxury Fever,* p. 45, citing *Business Wire,* "Credit Card Debt Reaches All-Time High Among Lower-Income Americans," March 24, 1997.

87. *U.S. Statistical Abstract 1998,* Table 802, p. 516.

88. U.S. Public Interest Research Group, "The Campus Credit Card Trap," September 1998.

89. Nellie Mae, fact sheet, "Undergraduate Student Credit Card Debt 1998."

90. Marcia Vickers, "A Hard Lesson on Credit Cards," *Business Week,* March 15, 1999, citing Nellie Mae.

91. U.S. Public Interest Research Group, "The Campus Credit Card Trap."

92. "Bankruptcy filings set record for 3rd year," *Boston Globe,* March 2, 1999, citing the Administrative Office of the US Courts; Mark Zandi, Regional Financial Associates; American Bankruptcy Institute website (www.abiworld.org).

93. Standard & Poor's, "Industry Surveys—Financial Services: Diversified," August 27, 1998.

94. Consumer Federation of America, fact sheet, 1998.

95. U.S. Department of Agriculture, Economic Research Service, Table "Farm Stats 1," website (www.econ.ag.gov).

96. Dr. Sally Herrin, Nebraska Farmers Union fact sheet, "Farm Crisis 1998."

97. National Farmers Union brochure.

98. Wolff, "Recent Trends in Wealth Ownership," Table 6, "Household Income and Wealth by Race and Ethnicity, 1983-95."

99. *Ibid.*

100. Gregory D. Squires, "The Indelible Color Line," *The American Prospect,* January-February 1999, p. 68.

101. Peter Medoff and Holly Sklar, *Streets of Hope: The Fall and Rise of an Urban Neighborhood* (Boston: South End Press, 1994), p. 14.

102. Dennis R. Judd, "Segregation Forever?" *The Nation,* December 9, 1991, cited in Medoff and Sklar, *Streets of Hope,* p. 15.

103. Medoff and Sklar, *Streets of Hope,* pp. 15-16.

104. The HUD statistic is 59 percent. Penda D. Hair, "Civil Rights," in Citizens Transition Project, Mark Green, ed., *Changing America: Blueprints for the New Administration* (New York: Newmarket Press, 1992), pp. 341-42.

105. Medoff and Sklar, *Streets of Hope,* pp. 28-29, 164, citing Alicia H. Munnell, et al., *Mortgage Lending in Boston: Interpreting HMDA Data,* Working Paper No. 92-7, Federal Reserve Bank of Boston, October 1992, p. 1.

106. Ted Sickinger, "When the door is blocked to buying a home," *Kansas City Star,* February 28, 1999. Also see Sickinger, "Hard-to-prove cases can be put to test," "Sides often keep bias settlements confidential," "Critics say regulators and laws too lenient," all February 28, and Chris Lester, "Minorities, mortgages and denial," *Kansas City Star,* March 2, 1999.

107. Medoff and Sklar, *Streets of Hope,* p. 29, citing Frontline, "Your Loan is Denied," WGBH-TV, Boston, June 23, 1992 and Peter Dreier, "Pssst...Need a Loan," *Dollars and Sense,* October 1991. Also see Randy Kennedy, "Suits say unscrupulous lending is taking homes from the poor," *New York Times,* January 18, 1999; Ted Sickinger, "Paying the price for a loan: Minorities fill financial void by turning to sub-prime lenders, often at a higher cost," *Kansas City Star,* March 1, 1999; Michael Hudson, ed., *Merchants of Misery: How Corporate America Profits from Poverty* (Monroe, ME: Common Courage Press, 1996).

108. See, for example, "Poverty Inc.," *Consumer Reports,* July 1998; Ted Sickinger, "'Fringe banks' eye low-income areas" and "Laws provide consumers little protection from unscrupulous lenders, critics say," *Kansas City Star,* March 1, 1999; Hudson, ed., *Merchants of Misery;* David Dante Troutt, *The Thin Red Line: How the Poor Still Pay More* (San Francisco: West Coast Regional Office of Consumers Union, 1993).

109. Melvin L. Oliver and Thomas M. Shapiro, *Black Wealth / White Wealth: A New Perspective on Racial Inequality* (New York: Routledge, 1995), pp. 134-35.

110. *Ibid.,* pp. 2, 152-56.

111. International Health Program, University of Washington and Health Alliance International, "Health and Income Equity," web site posting as of January 30, 1999 (http://weber.u.washington.edu/~eqhlth/).

112. John W. Lynch, George A. Kaplan, Elsie R. Pamuk, et al., "Income Inequality and Mortality in Metropolitan Areas of the United States," *American Journal of Public Health* 88, July 1998; "A Modern Tale of 282 Cities...Exposes America's Hidden Virus," *Too Much,* October 1998.

113. Cited in Gates, *The Ownership Solution,* p. 5.

114. William Wolman and Anne Colamosca, *The Judas Economy: The Triumph of Capital and the Betrayal of Work* (Reading, MA: Addison-Wesley Publishing, 1997).

115. Edward Wolff cited in "A Scholar Who Concentrates."

116. Donald L. Barlett and James B. Steele, "Corporate Welfare," a four-part series, *Time,* November 9, 16, 23 and 30, 1998; Citizens for Tax Justice, *The Hidden Entitlements,* 1996.

117. Senator Bob Kerrey, "Who Owns America? A New Economic Agenda," Remarks to the National Press Club, Washington, DC, September 17, 1997.

118. KidSave Press Release, "How to Make Every Child in America Wealthy, Guaranteed: Kerrey and Moynihan Offer Plan to Start Savings at Birth," June 17, 1998. KidSave supplements S. 1792, the Social Security Solvency Act of 1998.

119. National Center for Employee Ownership, 1997.

120. Gates, *The Ownership Solution,* overview of proposals on pp. 185-212.

121. Michael Sherraden and Neil Gilbert, *Assets and the Poor: A New American Welfare Policy* (Armonk, NY: M.E. Sharpe, 1991).

122. Leslie Wayne, "USA Accounts Are New Volley in Retirement Savings Debate," *New York Times,* January 24, 1999.

123. Citizens for Tax Justice and Institute on Taxation and Economic Policy, "1998 Tax Plan: An ITEP Policy Briefing," July 31, 1998.

124. Wolff, *Top Heavy,* pp. 33-59.

About the Authors

Chuck Collins is the Co-Director of United for a Fair Economy. He is a contributor to the forthcoming edition of *The Field Guide to the U.S. Economy* (The New Press, 1999). He was previously director of the Massachusetts H.O.M.E. Coalition and Director of Technical Assistance for the Institute for Community Economics. He has an MBA in Community Economic Development from New Hampshire College.

Betsy Leondar-Wright is the Communications Director of United for a Fair Economy. She was previously Executive Director of the Massachusetts Human Services Coalition, Executive Director of the Anti-Displacement Project and Program Coordinator of Women for Economic Justice. She has an MA in Social Economy from Boston College.

Holly Sklar is the author of *Chaos or Community? Seeking Solutions, Not Scapegoats for Bad Economics* and co-author of *Streets of Hope: The Fall and Rise of an Urban Neighborhood.* Her op-eds have appeared in newspapers nationwide including the *Philadelphia Inquirer, Houston Chronicle, Miami Herald, Cleveland Plain Dealer, San Jose Mercury News, Kansas City Star* and *USA Today*. She is a member of the board of United for a Fair Economy and has an MA in Political Science from Columbia University.